Simple Positive Play at the Library

Simple Positive Play at the Library

Jennifer Ilardi

ROWMAN & LITTLEFIELD
Lanham • Boulder • New York • London

Published by Rowman & Littlefield
An imprint of The Rowman & Littlefield Publishing Group, Inc.
4501 Forbes Boulevard, Suite 200, Lanham, Maryland 20706
www.rowman.com

86-90 Paul Street, London EC2A 4NE

Copyright © 2023 by The Rowman & Littlefield Publishing Group, Inc.

All rights reserved. No part of this book may be reproduced in any form or by any electronic or mechanical means, including information storage and retrieval systems, without written permission from the publisher, except by a reviewer who may quote passages in a review.

British Library Cataloguing in Publication Information Available

Library of Congress Cataloging-in-Publication Data

Names: Ilardi, Jennifer, author.
Title: Simple positive play at the library / Jennifer Ilardi.
Description: Lanham : Rowman and Littlefield, [2023] | Includes bibliographical references and index.
Identifiers: LCCN 2023001293 (print) | LCCN 2023001294 (ebook) | ISBN 9781538172940 (cloth) | ISBN 9781538172957 (paperback) | ISBN 9781538172964 (ebook)
Subjects: LCSH: Libraries--Activity programs--United States. | Active learning--United States. | Play--United States.
Classification: LCC Z716.33 .I43 2023 (print) | LCC Z716.33 (ebook) | DDC 025.5--dc23/eng/20230123
LC record available at https://lccn.loc.gov/2023001293
LC ebook record available at https://lccn.loc.gov/2023001294

There are many communities of people to thank for the creation and development of *Simple Positive Play at the Library*. I appreciate the experiences that have helped me grow personally and professionally and all the people who have contributed along the way. My biggest supporters are among my family—especially my daughter—who encourage me to play, explore, and contribute something positive to the world every day. I dedicate this book to all of you.

Contents

	Introduction	ix
1	A Look at Youth Services in Public Libraries	1
2	Philosophy of Play	11
3	Promoting Open-Ended Play	23
4	Structured and Unstructured Learning Environments	33
5	Participatory Design	39
6	Design Thinking	49
7	Collaboration	61
8	Playwork	73
9	Importance of Stakeholders	81
10	Assessment and Impact	89
11	A Simple Look at Programming	99
12	The Continuing Evolution of Simple Positive Play	111

Appendix: Photo Album of an Evolving Space 117
Bibliography 123
Index 127
About the Author 129

Introduction

"The mission of librarians is to improve society through facilitating knowledge creation in their communities."

—R. David Lankes

Public libraries are essential to public education. Even before the pandemic, libraries offered educational opportunities that supplemented classroom instruction. Now, with growing concern that students may have fallen behind in reaching developmental milestones due to virtual learning and their decrease in peer interactions, public libraries have an opportunity to enhance their role of helping young people engage with information and each other. Play is a powerful vehicle for public libraries to use to serve this need in the community.

"Simple Positive Play" is both the name of an organization and a concept for working with children in the community. As an organization, Simple Positive Play began with the simple idea that if the community found value in someone providing access to playful resources, the community would support the efforts. The first event in 2014 was hosted in a neighborhood driveway. It has grown to have a dedicated building and promotes family learning experiences in multiple communities. It is completely volunteer-run and funded by local donations.

A major obstacle that public libraries face is not only obtaining resources but also finding space to host programming and time for collaboration and implementation of programming. The concept of simple, positive play focuses on using easily accessible resources to provide engaging services that help young people learn and grow. It's about focusing on the details that indicate a positive impact in the community and recognizing ways to improve services. This idea is applicable to public libraries of all sizes.

Public librarians have the power to make a strong educational impact through youth services programming and collection development. This book serves to illustrate ways in which participatory design, design thinking, open-ended play, and access to resources contribute to an active learning environment for young people.

The story of Simple Positive Play begins with my relationship with libraries. I have a lifelong passion for libraries not just because I'm enthralled with good stories but also because it has always equaled a level of freedom and independence.

Growing up in the small town of Louisiana, Missouri, my parents allowed me to walk and ride my bike around town. Even though my parents didn't always have their eyes on me, Louisiana is the kind of community where everyone knows each other. My parents were fully aware of many of my questionable behaviors before I came home.

My three sisters and I always had to have a destination before we left the house. Luckily, there were plenty of places to go for kids with little money. At the time, it seemed we could travel all over the town, but looking at it now, we were never more than a mile from home. The longest part of our adventure was reaching the gas station to collect our snacks. Riverview Park was the next stop where we'd eat some of our snacks and hide them in our bags because snacks weren't allowed in the library. The library was just a few blocks further away. My grandparents' house was just a few blocks more, and there we'd inevitably get a few dollars to go to Dairy Queen. With ice cream in hand, we made the trek back home. Sometimes we would forgo the trip to the grandparents' house and go to the riverfront to throw rocks in the Mississippi River and wait for trains.

I don't recall any special story times, programs, or events at the library. The children's area was downstairs, and that's where we would immediately head after returning our books at the large circulation desk. There wasn't any staff downstairs. We were left alone to read and explore.

This is a story not unlike many others who love to reminisce about the days when kids could run around town until the streetlights came on. In my mind, I was allowed to do what I wanted without direct adult supervision, but the reality of it was that there was a community that helped me feel safe. I find it important to help cultivate this type of environment, and public libraries are the ideal institutions to support community connectedness.

My professional relationship with libraries began when I started working as a youth services specialist at the Florissant Valley Branch of the St. Louis County Library in April 2008. The St. Louis County Library system has twenty branches and hiring dedicated youth services staff at each location was a new practice. Previously, the responsibility of implementing youth programs was delegated to various staff members. There was also a Youth Services Department out of the headquarters location that would organize and implement system-wide program ideas.

The number of library programs offered to youth through age seventeen and their families had been limited due to the availability of staff to implement programs. In my position, I could focus my full attention on adding new programs and connecting to the community through outreach to schools and community events. The library offered a variety of training sessions, and I was eager to be a part of the various conversations regarding programming. The library system offered a staff collection of books to study regarding youth and teen services best practices, and I took full advantage of the wisdom offered from veteran librarians in nearby libraries and schools.

At the time, I did not have a library degree. My educational background was in psychology and communications. I had wanted to pursue an advanced degree but was finding it difficult to select a direction that would justify the time and commitment required. A master's degree in library science would allow me to advance to branch management positions; however, my interests remained with youth services and children's entertainment. I'd frequently check the job openings at places like the Joan Ganz Cooney Center or Fred Rogers Center to find roles that fit my career goals.

My fascination with stories and storytelling exists in a multitude of art forms, including theater, dance, music, fine art, and written and oral storytelling. The St. Louis County Library hosts programs featuring artists and live performances on a regular basis. Growing up in a small town without the abundance of access to such resources, it was rewarding to help facilitate events where young people could meet artists who shared their experiences of developing their craft. Although Louisiana didn't have the same kind of children's entertainment that was available at the St. Louis County Library system provided, I was able to perform in several theater productions, which instilled in me a great appreciation for the work and effort that goes on for a performer before an audience is anywhere close.

As the Youth Services Department for the St. Louis County Library grew, there were several more system-wide initiatives and standardization of programs among the branches. Participating in the system-wide initiatives meant more support from the communications department through press releases promoting the initiatives.

The establishment of a more cohesive offering of programs and services across the library system made sense to me. I was also new to the library world, so as some procedures were becoming more clearly differentiated for some, I was merely learning how to do my job. Change is difficult to navigate, and there were many instances when coworkers and community members questioned the changes taking place. During youth services training meetings, I would have conversations with attendees who would express their appreciation of the training but ultimately proclaim, "Well, that would never work at my branch."

I am motivated by optimism. When faced with a challenge to implement a new program or provide services, I immediately consider what I have and what I might need for my efforts to be successful, in some way. I would sit at the table in committees and contribute to the conversations that would influence program and service offerings, but "That will never work at my branch" was a phrase that would follow me everywhere. I attended statewide training sessions with presentations about libraries connecting resources to families and "That will never work at my branch" was paraphrased by youth services staff from rural, suburban, and urban communities alike.

In the summer of 2013, I came across the opportunity to register for the New Librarianship Master Class MOOC, or Massive Open Online Course. It was taught by Professor R. David Lankes through Syracuse University. This course was free and open to anyone who was interested. Lankes spoke about being a "guide on the side not a sage on the stage," and it helped me look at my role as a librarian differently. I learned more about the *Biblioburro*, who brought books to villages on the back of a donkey. Could I possibly be a librarian outside of a building? What would something like that look like?

One of the benefits of successfully completing the MOOC was a $75 application-fee waiver to Syracuse University's master's degree program in library and information science. I was accepted into the program, and in the summer of 2014, I completed the residency requirements for the program. In one of the opening icebreakers we were asked what we would do if we won a million dollars. I spoke about opening a children's museum in my hometown, Louisiana, Missouri. More and more, the idea for an organization began to develop.

The name of the organization had to represent what I wanted to promote, and Simple Positive Play was created. Shortly after I returned from my residency stay in Syracuse, my parents came over for a visit. I sat them down and shared that I had an idea to promote community and creativity. I asked if I could use their driveway and host a "Make Your Own" lemonade stand. I provided recipes for homemade lemonade and an assortment of craft materials. I also had refreshments available at no cost. I invited neighborhood kids to join us for play. I hosted a "Make Your Own" event one more time in my parents' driveway before I was invited to a new space.

The downtown area of Louisiana has many historic buildings and is located only a few blocks away from the riverfront. I was walking around the downtown area one afternoon and noticed an art studio I had never noticed before. As I was admiring the artwork from the sidewalk, a gentleman opened the door and invited me in. He introduced himself and then introduced me to his wife, the artist. After a short conversation, the couple recognized that they knew some of my family members.

The artist shared that she had a classroom space in the back of the studio that she had been wanting to use for classes but that I was welcome to invite families into the space to have access to playful resources like chalkboard blocks and creative tools like paint, Play-Doh, LEGOs, and more. We arranged to have a monthly "Make Your Own" session from spring to fall. I would pack up my car with as many supplies as I could, including books, and drive from my apartment in St. Charles to Louisiana, which is a little over sixty miles away.

After a couple of years, the artist had to move locations and no longer had the classroom space available. For a short period of time, play sessions were tested at the YMCA, but I wasn't able to host them at the same frequency as I had at the art studio due to scheduling conflicts.

In 2015, a parent who participated in library programs spoke to me about an idea she wanted in the community. The St. Louis area has many free resources and family-friendly attractions; however, these attractions are not always accessible due to location and admissions fees. Providing more opportunities for play in the North St. Louis County area would allow local parents a place to engage with their children and other parents without having to drive so far away from home. She and I presented to the Florissant Parks and Recreation Department, and they allowed us to use the downstairs area of the Nature Lodge at Sunset Park for indoor play. There was little supervision over this space. The park ranger would greet families upstairs, but the downstairs area was maintained, primarily, by parents.

In late 2015, we created a proposal to use an underutilized building at January-Wabash Park in Ferguson, Missouri, for Simple Positive Play. January-Wabash Park used to be home to the Ferguson Parks and Recreation Office. It now served as a storage space for cubicle parts, and the kitchen area was used for birthday parties hosted by the adjoining swimming pool. The city agreed to help empty the space and paint the walls. Simple Positive Play received a generous donation to replace the carpet and, in the summer of 2016, we were open to the public.

Beyond trying to obtain an indoor space for play, Simple Positive Play also promotes outdoor play and family engagement at local community events like Florissant Food Truck Knights and the Race to the Shrine 5k in Florissant. We've collaborated with EarthDance Organic Farm School to promote outdoor play.

Simple Positive Play is more than an organization. Simple, positive, and playful is how I view my role as a librarian who helps families connect to playful resources and build community relationships. When programs or collaborations are presented, breaking them down into the simplest aspects can help increase flexibility when it comes to providing a community service, no matter what the space. Simplicity also helps families engage with new material and information. Positivity is powerful and doesn't mean ignoring things that could have been done differently. Positivity also refers to creating environments where everyone feels welcome to explore. Playfulness is exploring the world around us and feeling happy. We all learn and grow through play.

Although I am a strong believer in the power of positivity when creating new ideas, negativity has a power of its own. The colleagues who shared that an idea or service wouldn't "work" had reasons ranging from lack of money, time, and resources to potential resistance from supervisors, management, and the community. One of my first managers and I had fairly good communication with one another. One of the first things she shared with me was that her interests and talents didn't reside in youth services. She had some experience, but her priority was thinking about the entire branch's needs and how it fit within the St. Louis County Library system. She was open to discussions about obstacles I was facing as a new youth services specialist and offered resources to guide me to more information. One day, we were discussing the disconnect between providing services for the community and the community taking advantage of the services provided, and my assistant manager joined in. Why weren't more people attending programs? My assistant manager answered with, "They don't f***ing care." On behalf of my assistant manager, my manager later apologized to me for that interaction, but it made an impact. I wasn't so naive as to think that prejudice and bias would play a component in my efforts but to hear someone say it so blatantly was jarring.

Over the next several years, I helped increase program participation and community engagement at the Florissant Valley Branch by developing relationships with local daycares, school librarians, and community leaders. I attended community events and started offering programs that better fit community wants and needs. Additionally, I received a grant from the Missouri State Library and the Institute of Museum and Library Services to implement a program called the "College and Career Colloquium" that encouraged students to lend their voices to the creation of new teen programs and a new dedicated teen space in the library. People cared.

The flexibility to develop and implement new programs became more limited as outreach increased and system-wide programs were growing. The St. Louis County Library provided a multitude of training sessions and resources to grow as a professional. There were moments when I began to feel as though there wasn't enough time to effectively do it all, even though I wanted to. However, I never felt more helpless or useless than when an incident in Ferguson, Missouri, gathered nationwide attention and the community I was able to serve was hurting.

In August of 2014, a young black man named Michael Brown was shot multiple times by a police officer and died from his injuries. He was killed. Protests began as people searched for answers, and chaos broke out as businesses were set on fire. Through tears, I watched it unfold on the news from my couch. I was checking social media to try to get a better understanding of the situation. The spotlight was on Ferguson, and all the viewers could see was a community on fire. This all happened before the City of Ferguson allowed Simple Positive Play to use one of their buildings. I remember being excited about getting a space for play. A little less than a year after the incident, I shared with someone I turned to for ideas that the space would be in Ferguson, and she told me not to follow through and said it was too unsafe.

In *Library Staff as Public Servants: A Field Guide for Preparing to Support Communities in Crisis*, the authors reveal that "public library staff aspire to support their communities but do not know how, or rush headlong to design to serve their communities."[1] This field guide was created during the summer of 2020 during an intense time for communities everywhere due to the global pandemic with COVID-19, but more crises were affecting communities because of heightened conversations about race, police, and justice.

When the protests in Ferguson delayed school starting in the Ferguson-Florissant School District, the only thing I could think of doing was more of what I had been doing all summer long. I asked my manager if I could use our meeting room space and I filled it with games and art supplies. I shared that I was at the library on Facebook as a way of letting some of the community I connected with know I was there and that the space was there for them as they were trying to figure out what to do. So, we played.

Library Staff as Public Servants addresses the importance of developing strong connections in the community before crises occur so that the process of pooling resources and responding to community needs is as efficient as possible. The field guide provides the four essential tasks of learning about the community, co-creating with the community, iterating and assessing with the community, and designing structures for the community.[2] This book will address these essential tasks in later chapters using anecdotes of Simple Positive Play to illustrate ways in which these tasks can be interpreted and implemented.

The upcoming chapters will discuss how libraries are an integral part of public education. Since libraries are embedded in communities all over the United States, there are many opportunities to be an influential asset and support the information wants and needs of the community. There are resources all around us. We'll look at how we can overcome obstacles facing our community by accurately identifying the obstacles, breaking them down into manageable components, and communicating to all stakeholders our progress using a simple, positive, and playful mindset.

The audience for this book is graduate students, professionals, community leaders, and anyone considering working in the youth services field. This book focuses on collaborating with the community to create an invaluable resource for the community. Without support, maintaining a quality space with relevant resources would not be possible. *Simple Positive Play at the Library* serves as a case study to challenge the concepts of how to maximize engagement with the library and even what makes a library a library in the first place.

NOTES

1. Mega Subramanium et al., *Library Staff as Public Servants: A Field Guide for Preparing to Support Communities in Crisis*, (College Park, MD: University of Maryland, Winter 2021), 4. https://yxlab.ischool.umd.edu/projects/reimagining-youth-services-during-crises/.

2. Subramanium et al., *Library Staff as Public Servants*, 4.

1

A Look at Youth Services in Public Libraries

The complete history of libraries is long and complicated. It includes the destruction, creation, and preservation of information through war times, regime changes, and moral viewpoints. One could spend many, many hours studying the various dynamics that led to libraries becoming an accessible resource for the general public instead of just a luxury for the wealthy. This chapter will focus on the beginnings of youth spaces in public libraries and the need for continued adaptability, reflection, and advocacy in light of the ever-changing information needs of youth in the community.

The pursuit for a more permanent space to operate Simple Positive Play versus the nomadic approach of traveling to community spaces, bears resemblance to some of the early iterations of public library spaces for children. In 1890, the Public Library of Brookline, Massachusetts, set aside a small, unused room in the basement of the library under the supervision of a janitor.[1] Although developing separate buildings for a youth public library is not a popular trend in the United States, they did exist.[2] In 1803, a wealthy man named Caleb Bingham donated a collection of books to Salisbury, Connecticut, to create a youth public library open to boys and girls ages nine to sixteen years old.[3] In fact, many of the discussions that had started in the 1800s surrounding the importance of a dedicated space for young people and the access and availability of age-appropriate resources continues to be a current topic of conversation.

In the nineteenth century, apprenticeship libraries were available for boys as young as twelve to encourage them to further their education.[4] The Youth's Library was established in 1823 by the Apprenticeship Library Association of Brooklyn. It, too, was for boys twelve and older but allowed girls access for one hour a week. Other access to libraries, beyond school libraries at private schools, came in the form of Sunday School Libraries where the collection included mainly religious texts. By the late nineteenth century, there were more leaders stepping forward to advocate for a more unified and integrated approach to public education, more specifically, the public library's role in the education of young people.

The American Library Association was founded in 1876. That same year, the United States Bureau of Education published a report titled "Public Libraries in Education." Young people and their role within public libraries were included in this report thanks to William Isaac Fletcher who authored a section of the report titled "Public Libraries and the Young."[5] This was a time when the public libraries were beginning to surge throughout the United States at the same time more care and attention was being paid to childhood development.

The combined efforts of several youth advocate librarians helped promote the benefits of spaces for children in public libraries through teachings and practices. Librarians like Minerva Saunders at the Pawtucket Public Library in Rhode Island began letting children enter the library at least fifteen years before most libraries lifted age restrictions.[6] In 1882, librarian Caroline Hewins of Hartford, Connecticut Public Library, began writing yearly reports about books available to children. In 1895, Mary Wright Plummer, librarian at Pratt Institute, is credited with designing the first children's library space that was intentionally built for children and not just a spare room or space in the building. Librarians like Lutie Stearns from the Milwaukee Public Library educated those in attendance at the American Library Association conference in 1894 about issues facing children of the time. The superintendent for work with children at Pratt University, Anne Carroll Moore, began training other library professionals by offering lectures pertaining to children's services in 1896. Additionally, Moore contributed to establishing children's rooms in every branch of the New York Public Library while she worked there.[7] These are just a few of the people who were incredibly influential in transforming the way the library can aid in meeting the needs of the community.

A major reason why public libraries were being established in communities big and small was thanks to the generosity of Andrew Carnegie. In 1881, he began giving free libraries to communities contingent on the agreement that the community would continue to support the continued care of the library.[8] The Louisiana Public Library in Louisiana, Missouri, was one of the first ten Carnegie libraries in the state and the cornerstone of the building was laid in the year 1904.[9]

By the early twentieth century, there had been a great amount of energy invested in the development of services offered to young people. The collaborative efforts between schools and public libraries became more complex as each entity navigated educational innovation and a changing community. There still existed a major disparity in access for Black, indigenous, and Mexican children. Schools for Mexicans and Mexican-Americans were segregated until the 1947 case of *Mendez v. Westminster* that made the practice illegal. Similarly, *Brown v. Board of Education* in 1954 declared that "separate but equal" was certainly separate but definitely not equal when it came to providing the same quality of education for Black children and White children.[10] These case rulings changed the resources available to all of the children in the community at school, but it wasn't immediately reflected in the desegregation of other public spaces like libraries. The efforts to be inclusive through collection development, services, and programming continues to be an area of focus.

During times of economic hardships, when library use increases, it also becomes a time for libraries to justify the use of tax dollars for the services provided.

The expansion of offering a library collection to young people didn't initially occur through an overarching organization. They happened in different communities over time with librarians working at the direction of the children in the community. As cited in *Introduction to Libraries, Second Edition*, Fannette H. Thomas's dissertation titled "The Genesis of Children's Library Services in the American Public Library 1876–1906"[11] found five conditions that contributed to the surge of youth services:

1. Specialized collection
2. Specialized space
3. Specialized personnel
4. Specialized programs
5. Existence of organizations and agencies devoted to youth

Thomas's five conditions applied to the public libraries during the early twentieth century just as much as it applies to the public libraries of the early twenty-first century.

The fifth condition of a children's library includes the existence of organizations and agencies dedicated to youth. Besides the establishment of the American Library Association in 1876 and the development of both the Association for Library Services to Children and the Young Adult Library Services Association, other organizations have moved toward intentionally focusing on the welfare of children with regard to education and literacy. Over the decades, since the establishment of spaces specifically for children within the library, there have been conventions and declarations regarding the access to information as a human right of children and the need for specific institutions to focus on the care and education of children. The United Nations Convention on the Rights of the Child was created in 1989. Support for the document is evidenced by articles within the Geneva Declaration of the Rights of the Child of 1924 and by the Declaration for the Rights of the Child adopted by the General Assembly in 1959.[12]

The International Federation of Library Associations and Institutions (IFLA) is a professional organization that was founded in September of 1927 during the Annual Meeting of the UK Library Association in Edinburgh, Scotland. It officially began operation in 1929 with fifteen members and has grown to 1,500 members and affiliates from all over the world.[13] The mission of IFLA is "To inspire, engage, enable and connect the global library field."[14] In June 2018, IFLA's Library Services to Children and Young Adults section published the second edition of a document titled *IFLA Guidelines for Library Services to Children Ages 0–18*[15] and uses information detailed in the Convention on the Rights of the Child to support its efforts. The details of the document reflect the same conditions of a children's library outlined by Fanette Thomas.

Part A of the guidelines defines the mission and purposes of children's libraries. The purpose of children's libraries being "to provide resources and services in a variety of media to meet the needs of children of all ages and abilities for their education, information, and personal development."[16] The document makes a point to include that the materials provided are also to aid with recreation and leisure. This aligns with Thomas's condition of having a specialized collection meant for children. The IFLA Guidelines document continues by specifying the need to promote information literacy and digital literacy in addition to encouraging children to be "confident and competent individuals and citizens."[17]

Part C of the *IFLA Guidelines for Library Services to Children Ages 0–18* also supports Thomas's condition for a specialized collection. Part C refers to collection development and management including making sure that there are materials in all local languages spoken in the community, created by local authors and illustrators and support local school needs.[18] The organization of Simple Positive Play incorporates several books by local authors in addition to some books that reflect the diversity of the community. However, the book collection is still rather small and could benefit from books in other languages. The majority of participants who visit Simple Positive Play are English speakers, but there is a population of Spanish and Arabic speakers within the community that isn't represented in the collection. This is not an intentional circumstance; however, that is not a good enough reason to not intentionally incorporate the insight of participants to develop the collection in a way that is more inclusive for everyone within the community.

IFLA's guidelines regarding resources available in the collection are not limited to the variety of books available. It also incorporates computer games, toys, games, puzzles, musical instruments and equipment, tools, and materials for Makerspace programming.[19] The organization of Simple Positive Play's collection resembles those incorporated by other local libraries like board games, puzzles, art supplies, and, of course, toys. Although, at Simple Positive Play, there is a greater emphasis on non-book related resources.

A space dedicated to children within a public library has gone beyond an extra space with a collection of books available to young people and their families and has evolved to include digital resources and technology like computers and tablets to help foster digital literacy. IFLA's guidelines not only propose having these types of resources available but treating the acquisition and upkeep of the technology with the same professionalism that is provided for adult technology services.[20]

What does it mean to develop a welcoming space for all children? IFLA's guidelines point out that different age groups have different needs. Parents of infants and toddlers could benefit from the inclusion of breastfeeding rooms and diaper-changing stations while teens could benefit from study rooms or spaces to socialize. The spaces are to be flexible to accommodate the different uses from story times to author visits and other library programs. IFLA does not have any specific recommendations as to the size of the space to be dedicated to young people as much as it gives a multitude of considerations when designing and arranging a space for young people.

The Danish Model Programme for Public Libraries is a tool that can be used to help design spaces for young people.[21] It was created by Danish LIS scientists Dorte Skot-Hansen, Henrik Jochumsen, and Casper Hvenagaard Hansen as a way to change the arrangement of the library from a passive collection to an active collection. The model focuses on developing a space that provides a positive experience and promotes involvement, empowerment, and innovation. These spaces aren't meant to exist apart from one another; rather, they are to overlap to represent the different needs and interests of young people at different stages of development.[22] This is not a prescriptive model but a tool to help define the different uses of the library for young people to others who share influence and interest in providing a dynamic library space.

Part B of IFLA's guidelines reinforces the condition of a children's library to have specialized staff. The requirements include a knowledge of children's psychology and development, ability to plan fun and engaging programs, understanding the culture of young people, and communication skills that enable a youth library professional the ability to identify needs and share information with children, adults, organizations, and other professionals whose expertise is beneficial to the implementation of services and resources in the library. Additionally, public youth library professionals need to have an understanding of the financial resources needed to adequately fund the collection, space, and programs. Because the library is such a dynamic institution, with the needs and resources related to child development ever evolving, continued education and training are imperative to stay connected to the needs of the community and the resources available to meet those needs.

Part D specifies the various types of programming that the library can offer for young people including those geared toward babies and toddlers, programs focused on coding and technology, and those that encourage creativity and imaginative play. This section also outlines the need to collaborate with other organizations that can assist in making sure that programs are accessible to young people with developmental disabilities and inclusive for families of varying backgrounds and circumstances.[23] The remaining parts of IFLA's guidelines refer to the marketing and promotion as well as the evaluation and impact of library services.[24]

Public libraries have transitioned from being a space not intended for children to an institution with dedicated spaces, collections, and staff. The competencies and guidelines listed for youth public library workers are numerous. Anthony Bernier, in his article, "Isn't It Time for Youth Services Instruction to Grow Up? From Superstition to Scholarship,"[25] describes the numerous documents available to provide guidance to youth services professionals as a collection of "aspirational assertions" explaining that there is little to no evidence to prove why the competencies are relevant and how it was determined that items on the various lists deserve to be included. Bernier refers to the work of M. Leslie Edmonds, who, in 1987, referred to the specifications of youth library work as being made on the basis of "superstition," which is a term coined by B. F. Skinner to mean "the incorrect assignment of cause and effect relationships based on chance occurrences."[26] An example of this, Edmonds writes, is if we solely believe that a good collection of material leads to good readers. In this instance, a library system might defer funds to focus on the collection development instead of staff available to provide readers advisory. If the reality is that a combination of a good collection and good readers advisory assist in the development of good readers, then the lack of availability of staff to provide the complementary reader's advisory service is lost.[27] Edmonds illustrates further superstitious behavior by youth public library staff by examining the time-honored practice of providing story times. Presenting story times can, indeed, be rewarding when participants are engaged and want to take the books home after story time has ended. The problem, Edmonds explains, is that the excitement expressed by the participants is an assumed value, meaning that because we did something, that something is good enough. This presents a challenge when we try to justify why we present story times to begin with. Is it just because it makes us feel good or brings enjoyment to participants? Or do story times provide value to the participants and the community? I can argue that story times absolutely promote early literacy skills, but how do we prove these facts with evidence? There is a fear, Edmonds says, that doing more research may reveal a cause and effect that goes against traditional beliefs with regard to children's services.[28] There's a sort of complacency to do things the way they've always been done instead of developing techniques to provide evidence that the effort we put into programs serve a purpose and make the library an indispensable asset to the community.

Edmonds states there are a few things that need to happen to improve the quantity, quality, and applicability of research in children's services at the library. One issue to be addressed is the attitude of those pursuing research.[29] Doing something different can be uncomfortable, as can discovering that something you put a lot of effort into isn't the best approach to reach a particular goal. This idea supports the "positive" component of the concept of simple, positive play. Every effort you make will not always yield the results you hope for, but it is important to remain adventurous and innovative in order to support the need for libraries and youth services in the community.

In order to conduct research relevant to children's and youth services, researchers need support. Beyond financial support, Edmonds clarifies that administrators at individual libraries should be willing to support and encourage research.[30] Edmonds goes as far as to recommend rewarding librarians who do research rather than simply tolerating those who embark on the endeavor.

The conduction of children's library research itself is one that needs further scrutiny. In addition to developing strong research techniques, Edmonds points out the legal and ethical responsibilities to consider when conducting research with children. Of course, having qualified researchers as staff members would be necessary to implement the research, and, at the time of Edmonds's article, there weren't many working at a library who were qualified and even fewer who were interested in pursuing research in children's services as doctoral projects.[31]

In "Isn't It Time for Youth Services Instruction to Grow Up?"[32] Bernier focuses his attention on the ability of graduate and undergraduate programs to prepare students to enter the library profession. Among other things, he delves into how the competencies and guidelines for youth library workers, or associational aspirations "emerge from rather opaque methodological process, without demonstrable grounding in evidence" and "without measurable outcomes."[33] Without a basis for why these different competencies are valuable, it is difficult to teach students why and how they are important, not to mention how to support the development of the skill. His research and analysis of syllabi ultimately conclude that there is still a considerable amount of work to be done to develop coursework for library and information science students to prepare for the ever-evolving environment of the library.

It is easy to romanticize the profession of children and youth services in a public library. There have been many times when I've been approached by community members who claim that they would love to do my job as a youth services librarian because they "love to read children's books." Although being familiar with the resources and services provided by the library does include reading books, it is more than that. Being a youth services librarian is more than cutting out crafts for children's programs or providing an entertaining experience for young people and their families. It would be a shame if we stopped innovating just because change is uncomfortable. If our argument for existing is simply "because we've always done it this way" we'd not only be wrong, because there was a time when all children weren't allowed in the library and it took a lot of perseverance and innovation to change that, but we'd be doing a great disservice to those who benefit from the services we are capable of providing. It is important to focus on ways to gather evidence to prove the impact of a well-supported children's library. It's also imperative that we share the impact to promote further research.

NOTES

1. Frances Clarke Sayers, "The American Origins of Public Library Work with Children," Graduate School of Library and Information Science, University of Illinois at Urbana-Champaign, 1963, 6–13.

2. Sara Innis Fenwick, "Library Service to Children And Young People," *Library Trends* 25, no.1, (1976): 332, http://hdl.handle.net/2142/6892.

3. Kathleen de la Peña McCook, *Introduction to Public Librarianship*, 2nd ed. (New York: Neal-Schuman, 2011), 242.

4. Sayers, "The American Origins," 6.

5. Sayers, "American Origins," 7.

6. Sayers, "American Origins," 8.

7. de la Peña McCook, *Introduction to Public Librarianship*, 243.

8. Stuart A.P. Murray, *The Library: An Illustrated History* (New York: Skyhorse Publishing, 2009), 183–184.

9. Louisiana Public Library," Historic Louisiana, Missouri, accessed March 7, 2023, https://historic-la-mo.com/historic-buildings/louisiana-public-library/.

10. de la Peña McCook, *Introduction to Public Librarianship*, 245.

11. Fannette H. Thomas, "The Genesis of Children's Library Services in the American Public Library, 1876–1906," Phd Diss., University of Wisconsin–Madison

(1982) as quoted in Kathleen de la Peña McCook, *Introduction to Public Librarianship, 2nd ed.,* (New York: Neal Schuman, 2011).

12. "Convention on the Rights of the Child," UNICEF, accessed November 6, 2022, https://www.unicef.org/child-rights-convention/convention-text#.

13. "Our History," International Federation of Library Associations and Institutions, accessed November 6, 2022, https://www.ifla.org/history/.

14. "Our Vision and Mission," International Federation of Library Associations and Institutions, accessed November 6, 2022, https://www.ifla.org/vision-mission/.

15. Carolynn Rankin, ed. *IFLA Guidelines for Library Services to Children Ages 0–18,* 2nd ed. (Netherlands: IFLA Library Services to Children and Young Adults Section, 2018).

16. Rankin, ed., *IFLA Guidelines*, 5.

17. Rankin, ed., *IFLA Guidelines*, 5.

18. Rankin, ed., *IFLA Guidelines*, 10.

19. Rankin, ed., *IFLA Guidelines*, 10.

20. Rankin, ed., *IFLA Guidelines*, 11.

21. Rankin, ed., *IFLA Guidelines*, 14.

22. Rankin, ed., *IFLA Guidelines*, 15.

23. Rankin, ed., *IFLA Guidelines*, 12.

24. Rankin, ed., *IFLA Guidelines*, 16.

25. Anthony Bernier, "Isn't It Time for Youth Services Instruction to Grow Up? From Superstition to Scholarship," *Journal of Education for Library and Information Science* 60, no. 2 (April 2019): 123. https://doi.org/10.3138/jelis.2018-0055.

26. M. Leslie Edmonds, "From Superstition to Science: The Role of Research in Strengthening Public Library Service to Children," *Library Trends* 35, no. 3 (1987): 509. https://core.ac.uk/download/pdf/4816833.pdf.

27. Edmonds, "From Superstition to Science," 510.

28. Edmonds, "From Superstition to Science," 511.

29. Edmonds, "From Superstition to Science," 516.

30. Edmonds, "From Superstition to Science," 517.

31. Edmonds, "From Superstition to Science," 516–17.

32. Bernier, "Isn't It Time for Youth Services Instruction to Grow Up?" 118.

33. Bernier, "Isn't It Time for Youth Services Instruction to Grow Up?" 124.

2

Philosophy of Play

Play is more than a frivolous activity that is innately performed by children. As adults in a classroom or learning environments like libraries, we are not only there to help keep the space safe or provide the tools and resources to play with but to observe and engage with the children to support their learning experience. The concept of simple, positive play focuses on recognizing the research regarding childhood development theories, the importance of play, and the logical incorporation of library services to promote an engaged and informed community.

In the introduction of her book *Theories of Childhood*,[1] Carol Mooney stresses the importance of understanding theories and childhood development if you're going to work with children. Her experience has come from situations in which directors were interviewed regarding their viewpoints regarding the use of theory in the practical world. The directors stated that people who came to the childcare profession with experience were more prepared to handle day-to-day interactions compared to students who had spent time studying facts about theories. She ultimately surmises that it is a combination of experience and theory that contributes to the best experience for children.

It is possible that some youth public library staff may share similar sentiments about learning theories regarding child development as the directors of childcare facilities. As long as participants are showing up to the library and using resources, who cares what anthropologists, psychologists, and researchers have discovered about the different stages of development? Youth public library workers support the growth and education of young people. Understanding the way that children learn and engage with information can contribute to the quality of library programs, services, and spaces for young people in a public library.

There are a number of books and resources available about the power of play and how to integrate it into the lives of children. There are pedagogies from the likes of John Dewey, Lev Vygotsky, Maria Montessori, Erik Erikson, and Jean Piaget that support the reasoning behind the existence of spaces that allow children to be the center of their educational experience while informed adults reinforce the connections between pretend or imaginary play to real-life applications. There are some distinguishing characteristics between each theory regarding play, but that comes from each researcher developing their ideas within different frameworks. However, the similarities between the previously mentioned researchers is that children need a safe space to develop problem-solving skills whether that be through peer interactions and language development or experimenting in environments developed specifically with the child in mind.

John Dewey (1859–1952)[2] was an American philosopher and educator who studied the US education system in the late 1800s and early 1900s.[3] One of the obstacles facing parents and caregivers at the time of Dewey's studies was the shift in the education system from children being more at home and learning from the day-to-day operations of the household to a school system that resembled much of what we see today with children leaving the home to be instructed alongside peers and guided by an educator. The role of the teacher, according to Dewey, was to observe the engagement and interaction of children and use those observations to "help children make sense of the world."[4] In education today, there are still parents who prefer to keep their children at home and homeschool while others send their children to public or private schools for their educational experiences. The amount of curriculum available for use in all schooling situations is very broad and quite numerous. Not all curriculum leaves time for observation and adjustment for each individual child's interest. As a public library, however, we are able to help parents and caregivers use resources to help balance the structured environment of school instruction with a more focused, child-centered approach, which can be viewed as playing or experimenting with information.

Play comes innately to children because that's the way they learn about the world around them. Every action doesn't start off as play or a source of entertainment, but anyone who has been around a small child who has learned that dropped items will be retrieved, knows that it all becomes a game. Sure, dropping something the first time might be upsetting for the child because they have lost access to that toy, snack, or cup, but one could entertain a child for several minutes by merely retrieving fallen items. It might not be as fun for the person picking up the same thing for the dozenth time, but the child will giggle or smile once they have their item back.

Jean Piaget (1896–1980)[5] was a Swiss psychologist known in the psychology and education world for his work on cognitive development. In his theory, people encounter four different stages of cognitive development starting with the sensorimotor stage at birth and transitioning through the preoperational, concrete operation, and reaching formal operation at around age twelve and through adulthood.[6] During the sensorimotor stage, children use all their senses to discover how things work. They aren't necessarily "playing" as much as they are becoming acquainted with their existence and doing what they can to satisfy their needs. It is a discovery stage. In the game of throwing things off of a highchair or a place to where the child can no longer reach it, it is hard to tell whether or not the child knows that they are the reason their item is no longer available to them. Once they figure out that it is a flail of the hand or sweep of the arm that knocks the item away, that is when the dropping and having the item retrieved becomes more of a game. It is only after an understanding of how their environment and body works does it become a game rather than a distressful situation.

Library programs for young people in this cognitive development stage may include offering a modified story time program called Lap Time or a Lap-Sit program. When I started offering this program as a youth public library worker, it was a small program that only occurred two times a month with very few in attendance. It eventually grew into a weekly program where there were so many babies that I had to change my opening song because singing each child's name would have taken up the length of the entire program.

I did not have registration for this program. Even if I did, it would have been difficult to stop mid-story or mid-song to check registration and question if a new participant was "supposed" to be in the room. While I understand the need to limit participation, especially now when we consider social distancing a common safety practice, at that time, I wanted to make sure that any family that found the program felt comfortable and welcomed to participate.

The design of the program included setting clear expectations. Who is the program for? What are we going to do? What happens if (when) my child cries? I consider the caregivers who attend these programs co-presenters. Children in the sensorimotor stage are non-verbal and imitate what they see and hear. If we, as youth public library workers, model playfulness and early literacy skills that are incorporated in our presentations, the participants will begin to join in. They will start clapping and vocalize when you sing clapping rhymes. This kind of experience promotes language and phonological awareness, or an understanding of how sounds come together to create language. The goal of lap time is to create an environment where caregivers can discover ways to provide engaging and rich experiences for their children.

The presentation of lap time included about twenty to twenty-five minutes of organized content and ended with free play time with an assortment of age-appropriate toys. One of my favorite aspects of co-presenting lap times with caregivers was listening to the conversations that would take place during the free play time. Parents would share their child-rearing dilemmas and offer each other advice and build a network of support. They would also spend time communicating with their child and introduce or reinforce vocabulary. For instance, a child might be handed a ball. The parent would say things like, "Look, a ball! That's a red ball. What are you going to do with that red ball?" They are playing and developing language skills at the same time. Week after week, moms, dads, grandmas, and grandpas would return and share the new milestones their child met since the last time they attended.

My role was to facilitate a program where caregivers could play with their children using fingerplays, songs, toys, and stories. The fingerplays weren't for the child to perform but for the adult to perform for the child. I didn't teach the babies songs and rhymes; I modeled actions and language for adults to use with their children and that their children could imitate in their pre-verbal, sensorimotor stage.

Erik Erikson was born in Germany in 1902 and began his education in the art field but later moved to studying the influence of society on the development of personal identities.[7] Like Piaget, he developed several stages of child development with the first being labeled "Trust vs. Mistrust," which is when babies form attachments to their caregiver. Erikson believed that trust consisted of both external and internal components. The external component relates to the way that babies trust adults and caregivers to give them what they need. The internal component is the child then feeling comfortable and safe within their space because they know that their needs will be addressed as they arrive. Again, this stage is illustrated in the game of knocking something over and then the item being retrieved. If no one picked up the item that was tossed and that initially caused the child to cry, the child wouldn't have had their needs met and the activity would likely never become a game. Erikson's interest in researching the way that society helps to influence a child's engagement with the world included the development of attachment. The library programs that are offered to caregivers during this stage of development reinforce the development of positive interactions to help children feel safe and secure in their environment.

Although there are general age parameters associated with each stage of cognitive development, Piaget considered that children would need to pass through each stage to advance to the next. The suggested age for participants in library programs always consisted of children at various stages of development. While the preoperational stage starts around two years old until seven years old, preschool story time was recommended for ages three to five and was a great laboratory to observe the egocentrism present during the preoperational stage.[8]

Being egocentric in this case means that everything the child hears, does, and learns gets related to themselves.[9] Preschool story times take on a different format than lap times due to the different developmental needs and capabilities. Conversations with these newly verbal young children can sometimes be confusing because I couldn't always immediately connect what they were saying to the conversation. For example, if we were reading a story about making a peanut butter and jelly sandwich, a child might chime in to tell me about their cat. Luckily, their caregiver isn't too far away to help me not only understand what their child is saying but also put that response in proper context. Instead of thinking that the kid just completely got distracted and was no longer paying attention, I could entertain the question and ask more questions like, "Oh! Do you have a cat?" The child might respond that they do, but I may still have no idea as to how that relates to the story of a peanut butter and jelly sandwich. It only makes sense when I understand that the name of the child's cat is Peanut Butter. Piaget's preoperational stage still relies on informed adults, or sometimes other kids, helping the child make sense of the world around them.

Erikson's next two stages of development overlap Piaget's preoperational stage. The stage that takes place after "Trust vs. Mistrust" is "Autonomy vs. Shame and Doubt," which occurs between one and three years of age. That is followed by "Initiative vs. Guilt," which occurs between three and six years of age.[10] These two stages are supported through youth public library offerings that include a craft or an activity.

Toddlers are well-known for expressing themselves and their independence. This is a stage when children are learning even more about what their own bodies can accomplish as they work to address their needs and explore using honed skills like climbing and running. The word "no" frequently presents itself in conversations with a toddler. Erikson suggests supporting children in this stage by providing opportunities for the child to express their independence while also continuing the supportive role of meeting their child's needs. The parent or educator can accomplish this by offering simple choices, not offering false choices, setting clear expectations, and accepting the changing needs from independence to dependence.

In a library setting, setting clear expectations helps the child and the caregiver who is bringing the child to the program. I am a fairly easy-going presenter during programs, especially with toddlers and preschoolers. I don't expect toddlers to sit on the ground and listen to story after story without mixing in opportunities for movement and interaction. There were times when a child would stand up out of their caregiver's lap and walk up to the book to point at a picture, see the picture a little bit better or, maybe, just to offer a greeting. Sometimes parents would attempt to call their child back or stand up to physically move their child back to a seat a little further away. Sometimes the effort of the parent led to more of a distraction than fixing any perceived problem as they would whisper-shout their child's name repeatedly or the child would throw a tantrum, also disrupting the story time. I have found that by making it clear what the expectations are in the beginning of the program, there are fewer distractions like this. I communicate to parents that my goal is for all of us, both adults and children, to enjoy the story together. To do this, we need to make sure that we stay seated or stand with adults, and we'll have time to talk and share after stories are finished and sometimes during the story. I share that I understand that this is a new skill for some of our younger friends, and I understand it is hard to sit still sometimes. I then offer spaces to go if a child needs to be noisy or move around and reassure parents and caregivers that I may ask for help if certain behaviors are distracting. It doesn't eliminate all distracting behavior, but it does set up a boundary and invites parents and caregivers to be an important part of the program. It gives all participants an understanding of the expectations and consequences if those expectations are not being met. The most important thing is recognizing that this is a learning experience and not imparting shame on the part of the parent or the child.

"Initiative vs. Guilt" is the third stage of Erikson's stages of development and occurs between ages three to seven years old.[11] While expressing independence begins in the previous stage, during this stage, Erikson suggests nurturing this independence even more. Some ways to support the child include encouraging their independence, focusing on the acquisition and progress of new skills, and setting age-appropriate expectations. Craft activities where there are options present to individualize the project are helpful during this stage as they encourage the child to make decisions about their own project. Incorporating tools like scissors to practice with gives the child more experience with the tool. Setting clear expectations in this circumstance might be to reinforce that we are learning during this activity and that it is okay if everyone's project doesn't look the same as each other's or as the sample provided. When we set up the program or activity to allow for experimentation, we're helping the child play and nurturing their independent development.

Maria Montessori (1870–1952)[12] was an Italian doctor who began researching and analyzing child development. One of the major contributions Montessori has made to the field of child development theories is the concept of child-centered environments. In 1970, when she opened a center for children in Italy, she focused on making child-sized furniture and tools for the children to use.[13] Developing a space where children have tools like brooms to clean up messes after themselves or knives to help cut their own food not only gives the children opportunities to master real-world skills but also develops independence.

Youth spaces in the public library can also help foster independence by having child-sized furniture that allows for the child to browse the collection. Additionally, online public access catalogs (OPACs) should be available at a child's height so that they can learn how to navigate the collection. Instead of a librarian or a parent using the catalog to discover reading and research materials for the child, kids can explore topics that pique their interest.

The third stage in Piaget's theories for cognitive development is called concrete operations.[14] This stage encompasses children ages six to twelve years old and introduces the young person's ability to reason and problem solve. Problem-solving is a process that involves encountering an obstacle and knowing how to use the right resources and tools to overcome them. Background knowledge in how to use a variety of tools and resources equip young people with the skills they need to problem solve. Experimenting with real-world situations through play in a supportive environment cultivates the ability for young people to persevere when faced with a challenge.

Library programming that supports this stage can include coding (with or without technology), book discussion groups, science- and art-focused programs, and more. Library districts with access to an assortment of technology can introduce new ways to engage with technology or offer the chance to work with peers with technology that might not have the resources, including space, in any other capacity. A concern that I've heard from other youth library public workers regarding technology is that they don't have the budget to incorporate technology. However, there are ways to explore computational thinking skills without batteries or plugs. In this instance, a facilitator best serves to guide young people through the problem-solving process and equip them with skills to research and find answers to their own questions.

Lev Vygotsky (1896–1934)[15] was a Russian who initially studied literature and became a teacher. Over time, his teaching experience led him to study child development and psychology, including the works of Maria Montessori, Jean Piaget, and Sigmund Freud. His theories focused on the idea that both personal and social experiments influenced a child's development. He is best known for his work regarding the Zone of Proximal Development (ZPD). ZPD is the distance between "the most difficult task a child can do alone and the most difficult task a child can do with help."[16] Vygotsky didn't specify that the help the child received had to be from an adult like a caregiver, teacher, or youth public library worker. The help a child receives can also come from a peer. Vygotsky also recognized the development of language skills and the opportunities to share information through peer interactions. Observations of these conversations can be enlightening to a facilitator. These conversations can reveal concepts that may need further clarification or showcase the children's knowledge of a particular topic.

As I reflect, one library program where Vygotsky's ZPD was clearly present to study was Minecraft Club. Minecraft is a game that either can be played on a video game console or on a computer. Players can construct worlds using blocks of varying strengths and abilities. This was a monthly program where the twelve computers in the computer lab were reserved for Minecraft players ages seven to eleven years old. The program was arranged so that all participants could engage with each other virtually in the same world. Although I was presenting the program, my knowledge of the game was very minimal. Fortunately, other youth library specialists had presented the program at their branch, and I was able to anticipate some of the challenges of the program. One of the best things I learned from my peers was to set clear expectations at the beginning of the program. Additionally, I incorporated the students into designing the expectations. For instance, what should happen if a person destroys another person's creations? We agreed as a group that the participant would be frozen or "timed-out" for two minutes. When play would begin, there were some students who had more experience in playing the game and would be able to craft impressive features like roller coasters or trapdoors. Sometimes other students would notice the build either in the virtual game or on the computer screen of another participant. Students would work together to not only show off what they could do but also to stop and take time to answer questions and teach other participants within the program, even me.

In the book *Jean Piaget: The Man and His Ideas*,[17] University of Houston Psychology Professor Richard Evans includes transcribed conversations with Jean Piaget. Part IV is titled "Interdisciplinary Research and Relating Piagetian Concepts to Education," where the conversation turns to applying Piaget's theories in the classroom. Evans asks for clarification regarding the importance of opportunities for young people to engage in self-interested play to help shape their own personal educational experience. Piaget responds by saying, "Yes, but it is important that teachers present children with materials and situations and occasions that allow them to move forward." He continues by explaining that children need "a mixture of direction and freedom."[18]

As facilitators, we need to have a basic understanding of cognitive development and our role in learning environments. Fred Rogers illustrates many great ways to facilitate in his television program *Mr. Rogers' Neighborhood*, which he hosted from 1968 to 2001. He was patient, kind, and welcoming, but how does that relate to play? In "Play is Truth" (2022),[19] Melissa Butler analyzes episodes in which Mr. Rogers's models behavior that parents, educators, and librarians can implement to create a richer learning experience for all involved. This particular article describes how Mr. Rogers utilizes what she refers to as the "space between the layers" instead of fast-paced action or a full episode of intense conversation about a complex topic like death or social issues. He didn't, by any means, shy away from talking about serious concerns that might consume a young person's mind, but he provided a space to think about how they feel regarding these topics. He showed us, as facilitators, that we don't need to have all of the answers for children, but we can provide space for children to process and create their own ideas.

Butler elaborates to discuss how reading a story and then combining it with supplies for creativity and a prompt can help young people consider the content of the story and stimulate conversation and thought. She exposes the fact that conversations about big issues are not only difficult for children, but it also makes adults feel vulnerable. Although we, as adults, might have feelings and ideas about a particular issue, it is important to have conversations where we let children express themselves. It is the way we can have genuine and honest discussions that affect our entire community.[20]

Dorothy Heathcote developed an educational approach to teaching that encourages facilitators to play. More specifically, she encouraged the inclusion of drama and imaginary play as a tool to engage older children in education.[21] Upon reading the title of her method "Mantle of the Expert," one might interpret the method to uplift the role of the facilitator and their knowledge of the subject matter. It actually refers to inviting students to consider what it would be like to be in a position of authority to make decisions. Educational experiences designed using Heathcote's methods consist of an expert team, client, and commissions. The expert team includes students who will work together to produce a product or program to satisfy the client in the situation. The client is responsible for setting demands, requiring high standards, evaluating the quality of their work, and providing feedback.[22] The commissions are the task that the expert team is "hired" to accomplish by the client in the situation. In *Mantle of the Expert,* author Tim Taylor explains that this experience isn't meant to completely take participants out of the real world to explore within an imaginary world but that it uses the imaginary world to make real-world connections and supports the need for more information using curriculum.[23]

In a library setting, youth library workers aren't typically responsible for children in the same manner as parents, caregivers, teachers, and childcare professionals. In my experience, most library programs only last about an hour. We may engage with some of the same participants on a regular basis, but that does not compare to the half-day or full-day experience other educational environments offer. We need to take full advantage of the opportunities we have to present programming as it provides a way to share resources and information and increase the awareness and use of available library resources. Inviting children to participate in an imaginary world that empowers them to make decisions and solve problems prepares students for Piaget's final stage of formal operations, which starts at about age twelve and continues through adulthood. In this stage, young people learn how to think abstractly and hypothetically.[24]

The age ranges for the different stages of cognitive development for young people aren't firm boundaries as to when a person will learn how to comprehend certain information because people present with different learning styles and situations. However, it can be argued that one does need the stage before it to reach the next stage. Incorporating theories of child development and the role that play serves in a young person's life into the development of library programs makes sense. Children learn by exploring the world around them and experimenting with situations through imaginary play and creativity. Library programs for young people should reflect the developmental needs of the young people in the community they serve by not only understanding and acknowledging the different needs for varying age groups but also by observing, learning from, and supporting what occurs during times when we are not facilitating.

NOTES

1. Carol Mooney, *Theories of Childhood* (St. Paul, MN: Redleaf Press, 2013), Introduction, Hoopla.
2. "John Dewey," Play and Playground Encyclopedia, accessed September 25, 2022, https://www.pgpedia.com/d/john-dewey.
3. Mooney, *Theories of Childhood*, chap. 1.
4. Mooney, *Theories of Childhood*, chap. 1.
5. "Jean Piaget," Play and Playground Encyclopedia, accessed September 25, 2022, https://www.pgpedia.com/p/jean-piaget.
6. Mooney, *Theories of Childhood*, chap. 4.
7. Mooney, *Theories of Childhood*, chap. 3.
8. Mooney, *Theories of Childhood*, chap. 4.
9. Mooney, *Theories of Childhood*, chap. 4.
10. Mooney, *Theories of Childhood*, chap. 3.
11. Mooney, *Theories of Childhood*, chap. 3.
12. Mooney, *Theories of Childhood*, chap. 2.
13. Mooney, *Theories of Childhood*, chap. 2.
14. Mooney, *Theories of Childhood*, chap. 4.
15. "Lev Vygotsky," Play and Playground Encyclopedia, accessed September 25, 2022, https://www.pgpedia.com/v/lev-vygotsky.

16. Mooney, *Theories of Childhood*, chap. 5.

17. Richard L. Evans, *Jean Piaget: The Man and His Ideas*, trans. Eleanor Duckworth (New York: E. P. Dutton & Co., Inc., 1973).

18. Evans, *Jean Piaget*, 53.

19. Melissa Butler, "Play as Truth," Fred Rogers Institute, accessed September 25, 2022, https://www.fredrogersinstitute.org/resources/play-as-truth.

20. Butler, "Play as Truth."

21. Tim Taylor, *A Beginner's Guide to Mantle of the Expert: A Transformative Approach to Education* (Norwich, UK: Singular Publishing, 2016), 14, Kindle.

22. Taylor, *The Beginner's Guide to Mantle of the Expert*, 23.

23. Taylor, *The Beginner's Guide to Mantle of the Expert*, 25.

24. Mooney, *Theories of Childhood*, chap. 4.

3

Promoting Open-Ended Play

The concept of simple, positive play begins with the idea that basic, available resources can be used to promote learning and aid in the development of problem-solving skills. Open-ended play and closed-ended play both provide value, but public librarians have a unique role in being able to provide open-ended play opportunities in a different capacity than other educational learning environments. Open-ended play refers to experiences where the activity can have multiple different outputs. The opposite of open-ended play is closed-ended play, where there are more rules and a beginning, middle, and end. Puzzles and books are examples of closed-ended play as are toys that are limited in their capacity to be used for anything other than its intended use. Although the books we use during programs like story times or book discussions groups are closed-ended resources, they provide a framework for working together in more open-ended ways. Effective facilitation of programs that allow children to make choices and explore based on their interest, instead of for a reward or grade, can increase the likelihood that they will continue to remain interested in the activity.[1]

Open-ended play is associated closely with the theory of loose parts by Simon Nicholson. "Loose parts" refers to material that can be used for a variety of different purposes like blocks, boxes, and art supplies. The theory of loose parts states that "In any environment, both the degree of inventiveness and creativity, and the possibility of discovery, are directly proportional to the number of variables in it."[2] Nicholson writes in "How NOT to Cheat Children"[3] that people often categorize themselves as being unable to be creative or imaginative and experiences for artistic and creative expression are reserved for certain people in our society. The loose parts theory can be interpreted as the idea that people will be more creative and explore more when there are more things available to use for experimentation. In other words, the more opportunities to engage with resources, the more creativity and exploration can occur.

The problem with applying the theory of loose parts, Nicholson explains, is that it is hard to focus on an actionable plan when observed interests are narrowed down too far. He uses the example of recognizing that children like to build caves and then subsequently creating a cave for children to play within. He acknowledges the value of play inside of the cave but encourages the consideration of play that can occur if children are provided with cave-creating supplies. The supplies represent the loose parts because the cave would no longer be a stagnant feature, but an evolving space developed through the trial and error of the children themselves. Developing a space where children can explore and experiment offers more opportunities to learn, which encompasses the essence of the loose parts theory.[4]

The St. Louis County Library system began a project to renovate all twenty branch locations during my time working there. This undertaking was incredible to watch as the library system hosted focus groups, provided surveys, and developed multiple opportunities to provide feedback so that community and employee wants and needs were considered in the establishment of buildings with more meeting room space, quiet rooms, and more colorful and engaging youth spaces. When the library branch I worked at reopened after renovations, not only was there a new colorful youth space for teens and children but also the entire children's space was moved to the large, underutilized space on the lower level. The lower-level children's area provided an opportunity for kids to behave like kids without the concern of disturbing library goers looking for a quiet library experience. The library policies still applied to the youngest of library users, but kids ask questions, laugh out loud, and sometimes cry, which can pierce the silence normally associated with library environments. There was an area for small children to build with blocks and engage in imaginative play in addition to a room that included large touch screens with child-friendly apps, a magnetic wall, light board, and furniture that could be transformed to offer a light, train, or block table. It even included a pneumatic tube feature where a generator pushed air through a series of tubes and people could place a scarf or foam ball in a compartment that would send the item zooming through various pathways.

Simple Positive Play the organization mainly specializes in providing open-ended play experiences at community events and within the building located in Ferguson, Missouri. Inside of the indoor space, there is a supply of blocks, dolls, costumes, art supplies, musical instruments, recycled material, and more. At community events, Simple Positive Play provides material like fabric, cardboard, duct tape, and chalk for students to have free range to create whatever structure or environment they would like using the provided materials. A cardboard box has the flexibility to become anything from a time machine or a house to a structure for carnival games or mazes.

The library system and Simple Positive Play both provide many variables for children to use their own imagination to create playful experiences even though the level of sophistication and budget for each organization are vastly different. Access to expensive material is a powerful attribute of libraries and organizations like Simple Positive Play. It allows for people to gain use and experience with a collection of resources they might not otherwise have access to for a number of reasons whether it be cost, space, location, and so on. These free spaces supply a vast number of variables for users and participants on a regular basis. However, do organizations sometimes "supply the cave" as described by Nicholson? Or are we supplying the materials for users and participants to build the cave? Are organizations satisfied with being viewed as a place of completed works? Or would it be more beneficial to be viewed as an entity that motivates and inspires experimenting, exploring, and discovering information? Using open-ended play and the concept of loose parts makes play flexible to employ in any household, especially when families have the ability to borrow material and variables from a quality supportive community collection.

Programming is an opportunity to facilitate experiences that help young people and families feel more comfortable exploring with loose parts and other available resources.

I've noticed that when families are familiar with libraries or a particular environment, they enter the space and gravitate toward a familiar resource or area. Those not familiar may enter the space a little overwhelmed by the choices available. Over time, they become more comfortable and open to new experiences. Programming is a way to invite people into the space and share possible ways to use the resources available.

My first experience in looking into open-ended play came when the story time group at my branch became quite large. I had started off with two to three families in attendance at story time. That grew to between fifteen and twenty families in attendance plus smaller groups of in-home daycares and two to three groups of larger daycare groups ranging from ten to fifteen students a piece. Initially, my story times would include twenty to twenty-five minutes of stories, songs, and fingerplays followed by a craft activity. When the attendance was low, cutting out circles, triangles, and puppy dog ears for each child's paper bag puppet wasn't a large time commitment. I even took it a step further and placed each item for the activity into a sheet protector. This was exhausting and frustrating at times.

We didn't have registration so, even if I cut extra, there were times when I didn't have a nice little packet for each participant and had to create extra pieces in the moment, which is not ideal. I'd have teenage volunteers cut out pieces for activities, but the quality wasn't consistent. When kids would empty more than one packet to get more eyes or more paper, I would cringe a little because I would have one less completed pack. Moving to a more open-ended play approach helped me to make more efficient use of my time and create a more positive and engaging experience for families.

When I was creating more closed-ended projects where everyone would have very slight variations, the idea of getting it "right" was very present. Parents and caregivers were eager to examine my sample project and focus their efforts on their child making replicas. I would witness frustration on the side of both the child and the caregiver when a kid wasn't focusing on placing everything in the "correct" spot.

I worked on presenting the activity in a way that encouraged creativity. Is there value in every kid at story time making a perfect puppy dog paper bag puppet? I am not discrediting anyone's effort at engaging students. However, I see opportunities for discussions about how many eyes a dog has or where the ears go. Should the long floppy ears hang high or low? What do you think a puppy is feeling when its ears are in various positions? These conversations before starting the activity would help to reassure everyone in attendance that there wasn't a "wrong" way to do the project. As a facilitator, I would provide the tools and a prompt and focus on a positive experience. There is a sense of accomplishment when your kid walks out of story time with a craft they are proud of even if you don't have a clue as to what they have created. In fact, asking, "Can you tell me about your picture?" can start a conversation that gives the young person the opportunity to communicate and share his or her thoughts. It's also a great chance to learn about the child's perspective and interest, which leads to opportunities to make more connections.

Focusing on an open-play experience also helped me select the stories I'd be using in story time. There are varying opinions on using themes during story time. I found themes helpful in many ways but sometimes found it challenging to find an activity that connected to the stories somehow. What skill or retelling experience could I help provide? By thinking of the story time activity more like an experience, I was able to broaden what I would consider making available to story time participants. I could read stories like *Extra Yarn* by Mac Barnett[5] and *Leave Me Alone* by Vera Brosgol[6] and then simply make yarn, scissors, glue, and construction paper available for creating. I could select *Press Here* by Hervé Tullet[7] and *The Dot* by Peter Reynolds[8] and simply provide markers or crayons and construction paper. At first, considering more open-ended play during story times made me feel as if I was taking an easy way out. Ultimately, it opened my eyes to multiple different combinations of stories and activities, and my time was better used by focusing on connecting the content of the program to early literacy skills and the other library resources.

If open-ended play influenced what books I was going to share in story time, the book *Reading Picture Books with Children* by Megan Dowd Lambert[9] has influenced how I share picture books in story time. In 2001, Lambert was completing her graduate degree studying children's literature when a course about picture books revealed the opportunities for discussion that the art and form of picture books provided.[10] Prior to this class, her interest in children's literature was mainly focused on the nuance of text and character development.[11] Through her coursework and eventual work with the Eric Carle Museum of Picture Book Art, she developed the Whole Book Approach to sharing picture books with young people.

The Whole Book Approach focuses on incorporating open-ended questions while sharing picture books as an effort to invite discussions with the participants. It is inspired by visual-thinking strategies incorporated by docents in art museums in which viewers are asked about what they see as opposed to the docent just explaining what is visible within the artwork. Reading in a manner that incorporates open-ended questions is known as dialogic reading. Lambert incorporates the analysis of the orientation of the book, the text, and how details within picture book artwork, gutters, and endpapers contribute to the overall story in the Whole Book Approach. Her approach changes story times from being performances to being co-constructed experiences with participants.[12]

The Every Child Ready to Read Initiative (ECRR) also strongly influenced my viewpoint regarding parent participation in story time. In the year 2000, the Public Library Association (PLA) and the National Institute for Child Health and Human Development released a report that analyzed school readiness. In late 2001, the PLA and the American Library Services to Children (ALSC) developed the ECRR initiative by examining school-readiness skills for the youngest of library patrons.[13] The emphasis was not only on what children needed to know before learning how to read but also on the practices that parents could implement to help their child learn. The first training I received focused on pre-reading skills like phonological awareness, print awareness, print motivation, vocabulary, narrative skills, and letter knowledge. The training even provided sample scripts to incorporate sharing this information within story times and why it was so important. It was a little difficult, at times, to shift from reading a fun picture book to sharing these pre-reading concepts while also maintaining the attention of the children in the room.

The second training I received shifted from the skills and focused on the five practices to promote pre-reading skills. These practices are singing, talking, reading, writing, and playing. This new iteration made it easier to be a better facilitator. That first training was rich with information, and it was intimidating to try to convey the six pre-reading skills to a group of story time attendees. However, the shift to focusing on the five practices made it easier to justify every element of what I was presenting. For me, everything could be tied into playing. We play with language and letter sounds through babbling and slowing down language through silly songs. When we play, we have conversations that build narrative and problem-solving skills. Incorporating age-appropriate books and stories together in a positive environment aided in print motivation and print awareness. The dynamics of my story times became the foundation for the programming I implemented for students as they grew up in the community and with the library. The Every Child Ready to Read initiative provided me with the background research to empower parents as teachers. It provided the opportunity to make the rich content of early childhood literacy more accessible to parents and children of all educational levels.

The Every Child Ready to Read initiative influenced the way I planned programs for school-aged children and teenagers, too. Reinforcing the same skills of reading, writing, singing, talking, and playing, of course, looks different for older children. There is a different set of expectations for older children. In school, they are presented with more closed-ended situations in which they need to focus on achieving the correct answers to math and science questions. The library program offerings shouldn't try to replace classroom instruction but build upon and supplement the educational experience and skills of older children. If students already possess the ability to read, it makes no sense for me to focus on the pre-reading skill of letter knowledge, but I can promote vocabulary, print motivation, and narrative skills by providing book discussions with student peers. This can become more playful when incorporating reader's theater scripts and puppets.

Programming for older children can also benefit from open-ended projects and the availability of loose parts, too. Novel Engineering is an approach to learning that encourages students to identify problems a character faces within a story and engineer solutions.[14] This approach not only encourages students to utilize their problem-solving skills but also allows them to "engage in productive and self-directed literacy practices."[15] Students and parents alike are attracted to programs that focus on science, technology, engineering, art, and math. Incorporating the novel engineering approach in programs for older children presents an active, hands-on method to share material in the collection with participants.

The training I attended presented the book *Peter's Chair* by Ezra Jack Keats.[16] In this story, a little boy named Peter must relinquish much of his old furniture to his new baby sister. His old crib and highchair had been painted pink, but his favorite chair remained blue, and he wanted to keep it that way. The facilitator I experienced stopped the book before the ending was revealed and encouraged us to brainstorm possible solutions to Peter's problem. We were then given time to engineer a solution and share before the ending of the story was revealed. After the story was completed, we then discussed how our creation was similar or different from the solution the book provided.

The two guiding principles of Novel Engineering were written with regard to classroom environments. The first principle is that "students of all ages are capable of engineering and their ideas can be used to inform their designs."[17] In my experience working in a large public library system, participants at library programs were not always from the same school as some were homeschooled or traveled from a different community to participate. This principle is very inclusive because there aren't any prerequisites to being able to participate in the program. Whatever background knowledge each participant possesses adds a different perspective on what problem to solve and how to solve it. Presenting open-ended programs that incorporate Novel Engineering reinforces the idea that libraries are environments where all participants can make choices and seek out information regarding their interests.

The second principle of Novel Engineering is that "teachers are capable of making decisions about their classrooms and their students' learning."[18] In the book *Novel Engineering, K–8: An Integrated Approach to Engineering and Literacy*, the authors explain why the book doesn't include many lesson plans or scripted scenarios for teachers to use as they attempt to use the novel engineering approach in class. The authors promote the concept of open-endedness on the part of the teacher and the students.[19]

Although the phrasing of the second principle doesn't include youth workers in a public library, the reasoning for this principle is applicable to the youth public library realm. The authors explain that this principle is meant to recognize that teachers are in a position to be familiar with the student's needs and are capable of adjusting a lesson that uses novel engineering to reflect student input.[20] Each public library is different, even if they are a part of a larger library district, and this second principle essentially recognizes that each learning environment is different. Novel Engineering empowers the role of the facilitator by providing the framework and encouraging those who choose to implement it to make adjustments based on their own background knowledge.

Previous experience in open-ended play helps with coding and gaming programs, too. Not every student has had access to coding and gaming resources. Some may have their own gaming consoles, tablets, laptops, and phones. Problem-solving with technology is more familiar to them. As a community resource, librarians help students to gain free access to experiences they would not otherwise have been exposed to. Not every librarian has the budget to provide enough computers or consoles to students, but, through facilitating open-ended play, young people have the opportunity to develop problem solving skills.

Adults in any open-ended play environment make a difference in helping participants feel comfortable with trying new things and experimenting. They also serve a purpose in helping young people make connections and expand their knowledge about the world, community, and their own curiosities. A study by Mark R. Lepper and David Greene called "Turning Play into Work: Effects of Adult Surveillance and Extrinsic Rewards on Children's Intrinsic Motivation"[21] sought to discover if perceived adult supervision changed whether a child would engage in an activity they had previously been interested in before being observed by adults. The researchers were able to determine that puzzles were a resource that children were interested in before the study. Some of the students were asked to complete the task in front of a camera that would either continuously watch or periodically turn on to watch the participant's progress. The rest of the students were asked to complete the task with no perceived surveillance that was conveyed by the presence of a camera that was dismantled and not facing the participants. In all circumstances, researchers collected data behind a two-way mirror. Another aspect of the study related to rewards for participating in the task. A portion of the students were shown a special collection of toys and told that they would be able to play with the collection if they completed the task. The other portion were not shown the toys or informed about the potential ability to play with them. After the testing, the puzzles were placed within the classroom as an option for an activity. The students who were under surveillance were less likely to choose to play with the puzzles as were the students who were told they would receive a prize for their participation or timely completion of solving the puzzles. Studying students and offering rewards seemed to influence the way the young person regarded the activity. Another study by William B. Swann, Jr. and Thane S. Pittman called "Initiating Play Activity of Children: The Moderating Influence of Verbal Cues on Intrinsic Motivation"[22] studied the use of tangible and verbal rewards based on successful completion of the activity. They found that verbal praise positively influenced a child's interest in an activity versus only tangible praise, which decreased a child's interest in an activity.

The studies mentioned in this chapter are only two of numerous studies aimed at determining what supports a child's interest and what becomes a task motivated only by the promise of a reward. "Competence and Overjustification Effect: A Developmental Study"[23] by Ann K. Boggiano and Diane N. Ruble included the effects of rewards on students of different age groups from preschool to elementary students and found that the motivation for each age group is different. One interpretation of all these studies can be that although adults should mostly stay out of the way of a child engaged in open-ended play, their observation has the positive benefit of providing opportunities for genuine praise.

Simple, positive play promotes opportunities for open-ended play that allow participants to have access to multiple variables that enable them to create whatever they want to create. The variables can be in the form of loose parts or through resources like books and toys. Open-ended play is flexible enough to incorporate into any environment and can be as simple as introducing a cardboard box as a play item. It allows students to gravitate toward what interests them. It gives participants permission to fail and try again in a low-stress environment. This type of experience helps to prepare students to conquer other challenges they may face in academics or other life circumstances.

NOTES

1. William B. Swann, Jr. and Thane S. Pittman, "Initiating Play Activity of Children: The Moderating Influence of Verbal Cues on Intrinsic Motivation," *Child Development* 48, no. 3 (September 1977): 1128–32.
2. Simon Nicholson, "How NOT to Cheat Children: The Theory of Loose Parts," *Landscape Architecture* (October 1971): 30. https://doi.org/10.2307/1128374.
3. Nicholson, "How NOT to Cheat Children," 30.
4. Nicholson, "How NOT to Cheat Children," 31.
5. Mac Barnett, *Extra Yarn* (New York: Balzar + Bray, 2012).
6. Vera Brosgol, *Leave Me Alone!* (New York: Roaring Book Press, 2016).
7. Hervé Tullet, *Press Here (*San Francisco, CA: Chronicle Books, 2011).
8. Peter H. Reynolds, *The Dot* (Somerville, MA: Candlewick Books, 2003).
9. Megan Dowd Lambert, *Reading Picture Books with Children: How to Shake Up Storytime and Get Kids Talking About What They See* (Watertown, MA: Charlesbridge, 2015).
10. Lambert, *Reading Picture Books with Children*, vii.
11. Lambert, *Reading Picture Books with Children*, xiii.
12. Lambert, *Reading Picture Books with Children*, xx.
13. Elaine Meyers and Harriet Henderson, "Overview of Every Child Ready to Read @ Your Library, 1st edition," accessed September 25, 2022, http://everychildreadytoread.org/overview-of-every-child-ready-to-read-your-library-1st-edition/.
14. Elissa Milto, Meredith Portsmore, Jessica Watkins, Mary McCormick, and Morgan Hynes. *Novel Engineering, K–8: An Integrated Approach to Engineering and Literacy* (Arlington, VA: NSTA Press, 2020), ix.

15. Milto et al., *Novel Engineering, K–8*, ix.
16. Ezra Jack Keats, *Peter's Chair* (New York: Picture Puffin Books, 1967).
17. Milto et al., *Novel Engineering, K–8*, 9.
18. Milto et al., *Novel Engineering, K–8*, 9.
19. Milto et al., *Novel Engineering, K–8*, 10.
20. Milto et al., *Novel Engineering, K–8*, 9.
21. Mark R. Lepper and David Greene, "Turning Play into Work: Effects of Adult Surveillance and Extrinsic Rewards on Children's Intrinsic Motivation," *Journal of Personality and Social Psychology* 31, no. 3 (1975): 479–86.
22. Swann and Pittman, "Intrinsic Play Activity in Children," 1128–32.
23. Ann K. Boggiano and Diane N. Ruble, "Competence and the Overjustification Effect: A Developmental Study," *Journal of Personality and Social Psychology* 37, no. 9 (1979): 1462–68.

4

Structured and Unstructured Learning Environments

One of the recurring themes when discussing open-ended projects is perceived lack of structure. While the idea of simple, positive play promotes play guided by participant interest, or unstructured play, it is not completely devoid of parameters, organization, or adult involvement. Adults simply take on a different role in the situation. At the building the organization Simple Positive Play uses in Ferguson, the kitchen area consists of an assortment of games, puzzles, and art supplies. I've had a conversation with a teacher friend who suggested that I have a central prompt for participants like a book with activity suggestions or a craft activity that is more closed-ended to help participants know where to start. I shared with her that I was reluctant to present these types of prompts because it seemed so limiting. At one point she suggested that I have a problem with structure. I disagree.

We encounter some sort of structure through everyday routines. There is comfort in the structure of our lives when we know when meals are coming, where we are going to sleep at night, and how we're going to afford the roof over our heads. School-aged children in traditional public-school settings are exposed to structure throughout the school day as they arrive at school, transition from subject to subject, and prepare to leave school. Some students experience even more structure through extracurricular activities like team sports, theater, dance, and more after the school day has ended. Many extracurricular programs, whether physical or academic, are guided by a coach or instructor, and kids are encouraged to build upon specific skills. There is value in a structured environment and with structured play. However, what does one do when the structure changes or a new structure needs to be developed?

On March 11, 2020, the World Health Organization (WHO) declared COVID-19 a pandemic.[1] Shortly after this announcement, schools and businesses began to close in an effort to reduce the spread of the virus. Some school-aged children started virtual schooling while parents started working from home, too. Some family households lost income due to job loss, and this led to other challenges concerning housing and food security. The global pandemic and shutdowns interrupted everyone's daily routines and the structure of how we operated.

The American Psychology Association published an article titled "The Serious Business of Play" by Rebecca A. Clay in May 2020,[2] a few months after the pandemic began. This article stresses the importance of parents incorporating unstructured play during the weeks and months spent at home versus in the classroom. Clay defines unstructured play as "play that isn't organized or directed by adults or older peers." Clay's definition continued stating that unstructured play "doesn't have a defined purpose or outcome."[3] Although the article communicates the need for unstructured play, this definition comes across as a little negative and can initially be interpreted as if playing has no purpose and that relationship building and stress relief aren't outcomes. Instead of defining unstructured play by what it isn't, defining it as student-led or child-led play would be a more positive description.

Overall, "The Serious Business of Play"[4] offers great, simple suggestions for parents to incorporate into the new day-to-day practices the pandemic created. It provides tips for pretend play and reminds parents and caregivers to let the child use their imagination with toys or things like boxes or blankets. It encourages adults to play with their child, or children, and create positive experiences. It is a very informative article that concludes with links to the International Play Association's "Play in Crisis: Support for Parents and Carers,"[5] and The Strong Museum by the National Museum of Play where parents and educators can learn more ways to incorporate unstructured play in the home and at school.

The "Educational Philosophy" for play at The Strong National Museum of Play[6] includes principles like making sure the learners are "active participants in guiding their own learning." The other principles I want to note include the acknowledgment that "teachers aid learning when they support inquiry" and that "learning happens best in a stimulating, inviting and nurturing environment." The "Educational Philosophy" also promotes play at school the contribution to physical, cognitive, social, and emotional development.

The International Play Association's "Play in Crisis: Support for Parents and Carers"[7] article provides helpful guidance for parents as they became even more of a primary facilitator of educational experiences for their children during the pandemic. This article stresses the interconnectedness that can develop through play, especially during a difficult time. Unstructured play gives children the opportunity to be in control and to express their feelings in a safe and supportive environment. Many times, the discussions surrounding play are focused more on early childhood development; however, the International Play Association states "Older children and teenagers may play like this, too. It is important we remember that older children still need time and space to play.[8]

In addition to home, museums, and schools, public libraries have the opportunity to be highly regarded for their contribution to supporting self-directed learning for people of all ages, especially young people. The public library is one of very few places where obstacles are removed to allow access to useful resources from a variety of physical resources to the access to programs implemented by library professionals that can help individuals connect to resources at any time of the day, beyond the hours of the school day. For communities that don't have a top-notch children's museum located in the neighborhood, public libraries are embedded in communities everywhere. Library workers are well-equipped to support unstructured play as they guide patrons on how to find and use the material within the collection. The more playful resources public libraries acquire, the more they, too, support the cognitive, social, and emotional development of young people in society.

There is structure to support unstructured or child-led play. The structure comes more in the form of creating the environment for exploration with the help of an informed facilitator versus an instructor assigning a specific activity. Public librarians and facilitators can model how to engage with young people and their creativity by encouraging problem-solving skills and without stifling imagination. The other benefit to having unstructured play qualities at the public library is that it promotes relationship building within the community. As much as child-led play helps parents connect with their children, facilitators can connect with families on a regular basis at their local public library.

In my experience with facilitating unstructured play, people sometimes seem a little uncomfortable. Some of the younger children cling to their caregivers, afraid that the toys are some sort of distraction allowing the adult to sneak out and leave the child in a new place. The number of resources is daunting. I try to ask if they have visited the space before if I don't immediately recognize them. Sometimes it is very apparent that the family is familiar with the space as the kids take off to different parts of the building. If they are new, I give them a short tour, pointing out the main playroom with pretend play and some gross motor activities. I also point out the makerspace area where there are craft and art supplies for younger children. However, that also requires strict adult supervision for safety reasons. Sometimes it takes multiple visits before adults enter the makerspace area. It is hard to know where to begin when confronted with a room of playful resources. Similarly, it is sometimes overwhelming to enter a public library and be expected to know what resources are available, where they are located, and how to use them most effectively. As a facilitator, or library worker, the job is to be a guide.

Simple, positive play is about creating a safe, welcoming environment and visitors having the expectation that it is okay to pretend, explore, and create. The structure of simple, positive play also includes knowing that there is someone they can ask for help or more clarification. Although unstructured play may seem like it is a less involved approach to education, the combination of structured and unstructured experiences support education on multiple levels and gives the child more opportunities to experiment and develop structure in a low-risk environment.

The maker area at the building Simple Positive Play uses in Ferguson, Missouri, has a supply of fuse beads, which are beads designed to fit on a pegged board and then, using an iron and parchment paper, the beads melt, or fuse, together into one piece making an ornament of sorts. The beads are mixed in a bucket, and patterns provide design ideas. The peg boards are in a variety of shapes like circles, squares, stars, and hearts and, while some participants work to follow a design template to create a bear, car, or peace sign, others just fill the board with random colors or develop a color pattern. Even though this activity can be done alone, participants will frequently work together to build one ornament. Either multiple participants (child and child or child and adult) will search for the colors needed and carefully place each bead on the board, or one participant focuses on finding the right beads while the other is in charge of placing the beads. Although I do have a few sample projects nearby to show what a finished fuse bead project can look like, I do not give a lesson on potential ways to engage with the fuse beads, nor do I assign specific project ideas or specific time limits. Participants don't even have to finish a project they have started. As a facilitator, I briefly educate the participants on how the resource can be used and then let them explore.

My ideal situation for simple, positive play is when participants arrive, the majority of the space is open and organized for easy exploration and not cluttered with past projects. There is a limited, designated space for previous work by other participants to serve as inspiration. Some participants will come in and move directly to an activity they have experimented with in the past and look for specific resources. Participants share with one another projects they have worked on in the past and then work together to create new projects either using the same materials or suggesting others to enhance a project in some way. My goal is to empower participants to use their own creativity and imagination to establish a structure that makes sense to that participant. The consequences of whether the structure is sustainable or a success comes at little to no risk to the participant. At the very least, the entire experiment will help the participant explore their own likes, dislikes, skills, and interest in an environment where it is okay to fail.

Creating Simple Positive Play as an organization has been a somewhat unstructured play experiment for me. My curiosity, background knowledge, and experience led me to ask if people would find value in having access to playful resources. However, it is more than just access, it's community support. Kids don't always have consistent structure in their lives, and caregivers aren't always equipped with the background knowledge or resources they need to support their child's curiosities. Community organizations like Simple Positive Play and the public library provide a service that helps young people hone their problem-solving skills to use at times when they have to create their own structure, when structure isn't available to them. Unstructured play environments provide children control when much of their time is controlled by someone else.

The concept of simple, positive play focuses on the idea that resources don't have to be expensive or incredibly intricate to have value. It is developing a space where young people can use what they have learned in other structured learning environments and apply that knowledge in creative ways that lead to innovative ideas.[9] I started in the welcoming and supportive environment of my parents' driveway, but not every family has the space or the support. Supportive community environments both structured, like in school or at home, and unstructured, like at the public library, provide families with a multitude of chances to learn and grow together.

NOTES

1. "CDC Museum COVID-19 Timeline," David J. Spencer CDC Museum: In Association with the Smithsonian Institution, Centers for Disease Control and Prevention, accessed November 25, 2022, https://www.cdc.gov/museum/timeline/covid19.html.

2. Rebecca A. Clay, "The Serious Business of Play," American Psychological Association, May 11, 2022, http://apa.org/topics/covid-19/children-unstructured-play.

3. Clay, "The Serious Business of Play."

4. Clay, "The Serious Business of Play."

5. Teresa Casey, "IPA Play in Crisis: Support for Parents and Carers," International Play Association, 2002, https://cdn.icmec.org/wp-content/uploads/2020/04/IPA-Play-in-Crisis-Booklet-for-parents-and-carers-2020.pdf.

6. "Educational Philosophy," Museum of Play, accessed November 25, 2022, https://www.museumofplay.org/educators/philosophy/.

7. Casey, "IPA Play in Crisis."

8. Casey, "IPA Play in Crisis."

9. Felix Reide et al., "The Role of Play Objects and Object Play in Human Cognitive Evolution and Innovation," *Evolutionary Anthropology* 27, no. 1 (2018): 46–59. https://doi.org/10.1002/evan.21555.

5

Participatory Design

When I first started as a youth services specialist, the library system was beginning to make significant changes to the spaces and services for library patrons. I mentioned in the introduction that I was the first employee with the designated title of "Youth Services Specialist" at that branch. The management team throughout the entire library system was changing, too. The director had just changed, and, within my first few months, my manager had changed. The assistant manager at the time would act as manager at the branch, and she had previously worked in youth services. When the new manager was hired, she recognized that youth services was an integral part of the services we offered and trusted me to learn the job with the guidance of leadership. I had experience in organizing information, customer service, and programming, but this was my first time doing all of it in a library setting.

The first job duty listed for the youth services specialist position was to provide programming for young people up to seventeen years old. There was a weekly story time in place; however, it had very little attendance. I was also hired at a time when an application for a teen spaces grant was declined. I was working in a completely new environment, but, luckily, there was a lot of information all around. Developing a teen space and improving program offerings for children at the library was a goal for the system, and it was supported through numerous training opportunities and access to resources.

There was a branch library assistant who had been working with local teens to develop ideas for the teen space. She handed over a binder full of surveys about the teen space and shared her experience with establishing a Teen Advisory Group (TAG) where I would be lucky to have one person show up for meetings, if I had anyone show up at all. I worked to connect with the nearby school librarians and other organizations that provided services to young people in the community, and I continued to research what a teen library space should look like. I also began to focus on how to not just create a library space *for* teens but *with* teens.

Eventually through my studies, I came across the concept of HOMAGO, and it made complete sense to me and how I thought public libraries could fit into a teen's life. HOMAGO stands for "Hanging Out, Messing Around, Geeking Out"[1] and has a focus on the way that teens interact with media. Initially, teens start playfully interacting with technology the way it is presented to them and eventually start tinkering with different aspects of technology. Eventually, they become more focused on a particular media and connect with others who share their interests.

In 2009, the Chicago Public Library (CPL) opened their first YOUMedia library, and it was everything I wanted the library in my community to look like. The idea of having access to a shared space with numerous people and tech resources like 3D printers that students might not have at home was exactly what I thought would be great for the community. YOUMedia encourages to "create rather than consume."[2] Although I didn't have the kind of space and supplies that YOUMedia had at the time, I wasn't completely without resources.

Teens came to the library, but they didn't attend programs. Many teens in the community needed to earn community service hours for graduation. I began using TAG as a program to invite teens to learn about volunteering and to provide insight about a new teen space. Another project I inherited when hired at the library was organizing the annual book sale and accepting teen volunteers, which would enable me to work alongside them to learn more about their wants and needs while also organizing discarded books and donations for the sale. The funds raised through these book sales were then donated back to the branch to contribute to purchasing new furniture for the teen space created in the library by moving and rearranging the books, shelves, and furniture that already existed.

Participatory design is also known as collaborative or co-creating design.[3] It is one of those things that we have all probably participated in at some point but were more focused on the tasks at hand versus what the overall structure of the tasks were called. Researcher Allison Druin describes participatory design in four stages starting with "user" and then moving through "tester," "informant," and ending in "design partner."[4] Druin's research in participatory design mostly relates to the development of technology for kids, but the process can be used as an approach to increase the use of library resources. In the example of the teen space development, I needed more teens to become users of the library before they could become design partners.

USERS

The user stage is when the participants are observed and skills are tested.[5] This structure was defined by Allison Druin's experience researching children and technology. In a library or community setting, the role of user belongs to those who are familiar with at least one library service. In some communities, people don't have access to computers, printers, or photocopiers, and they know that the library will be able to meet their needs. Many parents are aware that some libraries provide a story time for young children and bring their children to support early literacy skills. When I would give presentations to teens at schools to promote teen programming at the library, I would always ask them to name something at the library and many answered with "books!" Sometimes children were either eager to answer the question or looking to get a laugh, and would answer "table!" or "chairs!" to which I would say, "Yes! Absolutely. The library has resources like tablespace, study rooms, bathrooms, and air conditioning," because it does, and sometimes it is a good reminder that those resources are available if you need them. I would also share the other available resources like databases, DVDs, video games, and incentive programs to encourage more teens to come to the library.

Other than to get a library card, people don't need to interact with a librarian to use many of the library's resources. I can request a variety of items to be pulled from the collection and placed in a space where I can retrieve them and check them out without any direct interaction with another person. Library cards can also provide access to digital resources from books, magazines, and research, to music, movies, and online classes.

Community organizations like libraries need users because it shows that libraries have a purpose for existing and deserve support. The organization of Simple Positive Play expanded because people kept showing up and it gathered the attention of others who wanted to support the free access to a shared collection of resources. As the relationship between an organization and users grows, it leads to more opportunities for users to become testers by communicating input.

TESTERS

According to Druin, a "tester" is someone who provides direct feedback about their experience.[6] Opportunities for feedback contribute more information to help library professionals design services. In Druin's research about educational technology for children, changes to the technology were often made for the ease of the parents and teachers and not for the actual users of the technology, the children. Since youth services is a position to provide services to young people, allowing them a way to deliver feedback gives them a voice in a conversation about what affects them.

Within my first year of employment, I submitted an application for the Targeted Populations Grant supported by the Institute of Museum and Library Services under the provisions of the Library Services and Technology Act as administered by the Missouri State Library, a division of the Office of the Secretary of State. My project was titled the "Teen Library Challenge: Preparing Teens for Community, Careers and College." This project consisted of a guest speaker, several workshops, and a competition for teens to contribute to the library. The workshops were in collaboration with a local organization called the Scholarship Foundation, which offered interview tips and also available showed some of the professional attire available at its resale shop called the ScholarShop.

The competition aspect of the program included designing a new way to improve promotion of library services, enhance teen programs, or develop physical space of the teen area. Students had to complete an application that included a short essay answer to "Is it important for a public library to provide programming and workshops for teens? Why or why not?" Students also had to complete a project-specific proposal and interview with myself and my manager about their idea. After receiving input from teens at other programs and consulting with my manager about the proposed projects, a winner was selected and given a prize of a laptop computer.

This program was primarily designed by adults, and it provided the chance to collaborate with other organizations and get feedback from teens in the community. The goal was to get at least thirty students to participate in the Teen Library Challenge; however, the final number of students to make it to the end was five. Three of the proposals regarded programs, one focused on promotion while the third addressed the twenty-five-square-foot space available to use at a dedicated teen area within the library. Although one of the program proposals won the competition, the other proposals influenced future efforts to connect with the teen population.

INFORMANTS

Informants contribute at various stages of the development of the technology.[7] The "Teen Library Challenge" could have looked completely different if teens were more involved in the creation of the program. As we started to design the newly created teen space, there were more teens involved on a monthly basis. They were given samples of carpet and furniture to choose from and made choices regarding the color of the paint for the walls and pillars. Teens became informants on a more regular basis as we consulted them on a more regular basis when we scheduled large projects like programs with the Summer Reading Club program.

One of the components of including informants is the use of low-tech materials and meeting more frequently. In this stage, participants are investing more of their time and energy, building stronger relationships with others, and becoming more familiar with the low-tech materials supplied.

In a library and community setting, this looks like effectively using the resources that are currently available for that age group to support the need for more or different resources in the future. It presents the chance to take ownership within the library as facilitators encourage creative thinking and problem-solving skills. Programs that invite participants to share their interests present a platform for young people to use their voice to influence a community resource that welcomes their input.

DESIGN PARTNERS

Instead of designing a particular technology or product, design partners in a library setting are very involved with shaping the library collection and services. We want youth users to become design partners, and by presenting more programs based upon their interests, libraries and community resources present themselves as valuable resources.

The variety and amount of resources, including the time of the staff member assigned or dedicated to serving young people, varies from community to community. Focusing on becoming design partners with young people helped alleviate some of the pressure of creating a program that increases library usage. I spent less time guessing what library users would find appealing and focused more on implementing programs that met interests and needs.

The public library is one of the only places where a young person can have their own membership card and independently explore subjects that interest them. It is a place where people of all economic statuses have the same access to the same material within a particular library or library system. As a youth services librarian, I get to help connect and inform users to information, invite feedback and develop an engaging environment for learning and building relationships.

There are a few discoveries in Druin's research regarding the difference in engaging with participatory design with adults and children. Some of the considerations include things like how adults and children introduce themselves, how they interact within the setting, their style of dress, and compensation.[8]

The power structure within most adult-child situations is one in which the adult is in charge and the child is to follow the lead and direction of the adult. However, in participatory design with children, the situation needs to strive to be one where adults and children are treated as equal partners with valuable ideas to contribute.

One method Druin proposes for creating a group of equal partners with adults and children is to encourage all group members to refer to each other by their first name.[9] This can be a difficult behavior to achieve for several reasons, with a prominent one being cultural differences. In my family, I was never to refer to an adult by their first name to the point where, even today, I refer to former teachers and parents of friends as their proper title and last name. When I first started working at the library, I would introduce myself as my first name and parents would always add a "Miss" as my title. Some parents would go as far as to ask my last name and encourage their child to call me Miss Richardson or, later, Mrs. Ilardi. To be honest, using my last name always made me a little uncomfortable because it seemed so formal. It wasn't my preferred way of being addressed, but I understood the reasoning behind it because it resembled my own upbringing. Being able to call an adult by their first name changes the dynamic of the relationship between the adult and the child.

Druin also suggested that all participants refrain from raising their hands when contributing an idea to a conversation.[10] In a classroom setting, raising your hand to answer a question or make a comment is common practice. An instructor then calls on the student, giving the student permission to speak. Being in an environment where everyone is expected to listen and wait for an opportunity to speak, especially an environment with adults and children, can also be a new experience for some participants.

The other two methods for helping adults and children view each other as equal partners are a little difficult to envision in a library environment. These expectations include the type of clothing the adults wear and the compensation each participant receives. Druin encourages adults to dress in informal attire that doesn't contribute to reinforcing the idea that the adult is in charge of the young people of the group. She also makes sure that all participants, adults and children, are compensated in some capacity for their time, with children being paid with a yearly technology gift.[11]

Setting these types of expectations while trying to engage in participatory design as a youth public library worker would be a difficult undertaking. Although I would frequently get the same participants in a program, the attendance often consisted of different attendees from session to session. Library programs that occurred as a series were also difficult to retain the same attendees from session to session due to the time commitment not just for the participants but also for the caregivers bringing the participants to the program. The main tool that youth public libraries have to work with is their own consistency of expectations within every program. From there, a culture of actively participating in programs can be developed with attendees starting as users and then moving to becoming informants, testers, and then design partners.

In my experience working at a public library, there wasn't a separate dress code for youth library workers and the rest of the library staff. We were only allowed to dress in informal wear by wearing jeans on certain days or for special projects. Expecting a youth public library worker to change clothes for every role they adopt throughout a workday would be a cumbersome task and lead to spending more time making costume changes than implementing the variety of work being done on any given day. Being presentable and approachable while also being able to carry out daily tasks should be the main priority.

Raising one's hand to speak is an etiquette practiced by adults and young people alike. In group meetings or brainstorming sessions, indicating that you have something to add to the conversation by raising a hand or making some sort of physical gesture is common practice, in my experience. Learning how to wait for your turn to speak is a skill. Otherwise, people will talk over each other and no one's ideas can be clearly heard or understood. The reasoning behind the expectation to not raise hands for Druin is that it "enables all to contribute without asking permission."[12] More than the actual act of raising a hand, the environment for participatory design with children needs to be established in a way where children feel like their contributions are valuable. No one wants to be put on the spot to potentially embarrass themselves with the wrong answer. There is a saying that goes, "There are no stupid questions." Expressing this statement out loud to a group is sometimes met with students accepting the challenge of asking absurd questions. However, a facilitator can express the importance of listening to other participants' contributions to the conversation and then guiding them to engage in a group project. Druin proposed doing this by discovering commonalities within the group and engaging in collaborative design projects that allowed participants to tackle solving a problem they encounter whether it is opening a milk carton or changing something within the classroom.[13] For the library, consistently implementing programs that promote open-ended results equips all participants with the experience of contributing their own thoughts and ideas to a project.

The concept of compensation for both adults and young people in projects and services that incorporate participatory design is somewhat easy to discuss considering that all, or most, library programs are free to all participants.

Offering a reward for participating in a library program that it implemented regularly doesn't seem like a sustainable practice. However, offering recognition and praise by sharing the creativity exhibited in programs with others either through a display or pictures on social media can be rewarding for participants and showcase the environment established within library programs.

While Druin worked with adults and children using participatory design to create new technologies, Mega Subramaniam and Linda W. Braun used participatory design to engage with 137 public librarians to determine how the library was helping non-dominant youth and their families during a time of a global pandemic and civil unrest.[14] Subramaniam and Braun conducted their research during May 2020 and August 2020, and their findings yielded a field guide to help public librarians co-create solutions to challenges facing the community. One of the prevalent notions that entered their research was the idea of public librarians serving in more of a "library servant" capacity versus a "public servant" capacity. The difference between these two terms is that a "library servant" knows what is best for current and potential library users without the added step of asking users about their needs. A "public servant," on the other hand, collaborates with current and potential users to have conversations and co-design methods for addressing the needs of the community using the resources available through the public library.

Braun and Subramanium hosted several participatory design sessions and conducted interviews with public librarians to gather further insight regarding the challenges that public librarians were facing during a time when library buildings were not open to the public and the traditional approaches to engaging with the community were suspended. They ultimately discovered that public librarians need to have the skills to collaborate with the community so that in times of crisis, libraries and librarians remain sources of information that meet the needs of the community.[15] As a result of their project, they developed a Field Guide for public librarians that includes learning about the community, co-creating with the community, properly assessing the programs and services implemented, and adapting the structure of the library to reflect the needs of the community.[16]

The concept of simple, positive play stresses the importance of the use of play to learn. Play isn't just a concept that can be applied as a children's activity but one that we can keep in mind when working with others. For example, if a child brings a baseball and a bat to a playground and insists on dictating every way the other kids play, it can lead to children no longer wanting to play baseball with that child. However, by providing some equipment to play baseball, the framework for engaging in the activity is established, but everyone can play using their individual talents and skills. By recognizing that the library is a valuable entity with access to information and resources for the community, we're supplying the material, but we can also collaborate with the community to help them use it to meet community needs. Participatory Design is a way to invite the community to play.

NOTES

1. "What is HOMAGO?" YOUMedia Learning Labs Network, accessed July 19, 2022, https://youmedia.org/about/homago/.
2. "YOUmedia," Chicago Public Library, accessed July 19, 2022, https://www.chipublib.org/programs-and-partnerships/youmedia/.
3. Olga Elizarova and Kimberly Dowd, "Participatory Design in Practice," UX Magazine, October 14, 2017, https://uxmag.com/articles/participatory-design-in-practice.
4. Allison Druin, "The Role of Children in the Design of New Technology," *Behaviour and Information Technology (BIT)* 27, no. 1 (2002): 1. https://doi.org/10.1080/01449290110108659.
5. Druin, "The Role of Children in the Design of New Technology," 5.
6. Druin, "The Role of Children in the Design of New Technology," 9.
7. Druin, "The Role of Children in the Design of New Technology," 10.
8. Druin, "The Role of Children and the Design of New Technology," 21.
9. Druin, "The Role of Children and the Design of New Technology," 21.
10. Druin, "The Role of Children and the Design of New Technology," 21.
11. Druin, "The Role of Children and the Design of New Technology," 21.
12. Druin, "The Role of Children and the Design of New Technology," 21.
13. Druin, "The Role of Children and the Design of New Technology," 21.
14. Mega Subramaniam and Linda W. Braun, "Changing the Mindset of Pre-Service Librarians: Moving from Library Servants to Public Servants," IDEALS, ALISE 2021 Juried Papers, published September 20, 2021, http://hdl.handle.net/2142/11093.
15. Subramanium and Braun, "Changing the Mindset of Pre-Service Librarians."
16. Mega Subramaniam et al., "Library Staff as Public Servants: A Field Guide for Preparing to Support Communities in Crisis," (Winter 2021), http://https://yxlab.ischool.umd.edu/projects/reimagining-youth-services-during-crises/.

6

Design Thinking

Design thinking is where the previous chapters about connected learning, libraries, open-ended play, and unstructured play come together. It is where the concept of simple, positive play comes together to create programs and services that meet community needs.

Design thinking is a problem-solving method that can be used by librarians to create positive community experiences. The five main stages identified in the process are empathize, define, ideate, prototype, and test. Empathizing includes getting a firm understanding of the community in order to identify obstacles that can potentially be removed through programs and services. Defining is the stage in which the problem you are looking to solve is clearly identified. The stage of ideation is when brainstorming takes place and work is done to develop possible solutions to the identified problem. Prototyping is creating a tangible representation of the solution. Then, it becomes time to test out the idea to see how it works.

It seems to be a fairly simple five-stage process, but there are ways to become more proficient and effective at each of the stages when each stage is examined more thoroughly. IDEO created a Design Thinking for Libraries Toolkit[1] that explains design thinking as three phases: inspiration, ideation, and iteration. The five stages previously mentioned occur within each of these phases. There are resources to help those interested in design thinking to facilitate workshops about the different stages. However, even after taking a course or utilizing a toolkit, learning and utilizing design thinking skills isn't a one-time occurrence. It's an iterative process that involves constant reflection and assessment.[2]

In January through March of 2018, Rachel Ivy Clarke, Ann Rosenblad, and Satyen Amonkar[3] conducted a survey in which they asked library workers questions about design thinking. Out of the 284 surveys received, 12 were discarded due to the respondents not currently working within a library and 145 out of the remaining 272 surveys were completed in their entirety. Many of the respondents (50 percent) identified as being employed in an administrative position, and the average number of years of library work was eighteen. From this survey, Clarke et al. were able to receive feedback regarding the use of design thinking within the library, and the results provided insight for anyone looking to incorporate design thinking at their library.

Some of the respondents were not familiar with the concept of design thinking. The researchers in the study posited that the reason why some of the surveys weren't completed was due to the questions specifically regarding design-thinking skills included on the survey. The final results indicated that three-fourths of those surveyed considered design thinking relevant to children's and teen services; however, none of the respondents who identified as young adult services were very familiar with design thinking.

The survey included opportunities for open-ended feedback regarding design thinking, and not all of it was positive. Some respondents shared negative experiences with design-thinking criticisms of design thinking discovered through the study. A highlighted result in the study was that the majority of those who identified as young adult services answered they were not familiar with the term. There were some respondents who didn't consider design thinking a necessary requirement for graduate education in library and information science but recommended that it be offered as an elective.

The study reveals that there is a disconnect between learning about design thinking and applying it to the work done in libraries. When studying through the Youth Experience Program (YX) at the University of Maryland, I found the process a little messy, myself. We were learning about design thinking, participatory design, computational thinking, and more. The research was fascinating, and I worked very hard. It was sometimes difficult to work on assignments that put us, the students, in real-time library situations. For instance, trying to plan a series of programs to illustrate the skills we learned was hard to align with existing deadlines and branch expectations. As frustrating as it sometimes was, it gave me a new perspective toward the many aspects regarding a young person's experience with the library. In the end, I was able to develop a monthly program called Tech Tuesday where I was able to engage students with no-tech/low-tech open-ended projects.

Another positive aspect of the YX program, beyond opportunities to enhance the impact I can have through programming, was the ability to work with other individuals in the program from across the United States who were also dealing with similar obstacles. I had other people to help brainstorm and troubleshoot solutions. It was an extremely informative experience to collaborate with other students for presentations at the Young Adult Library Services Association (YALSA). The overall support in the program was abundant, and, even though it was challenging, it was an experience that continues to shape the way I use design thinking in some stage or phase every day.

One section of the study was dedicated to the "Fear of Commercialism."[4] Some librarians who took part in the survey believed that design-thinking skills and the design-thinking process was used by corporations and businesses to sell products to a consumer and, therefore, something to be wary of. All programs and services should be examined with a critical eye. Library workers are, indeed, selling something. We sell the idea that people benefit from having free access to shared resources.

Sometimes learning about different techniques to engage with families and increase access and usability of free resources becomes overcomplicated. I'm not promoting flippant, random choices to implement a program or service but a more focused attention on efficiently using currently available resources, skills, and abilities to reach organizational goals. There is always room for growth and building on existing structures, but it all has to start somewhere. Making an extravagant plan that doesn't get implemented until you have accounted for every potential obstacle can be prohibitive to progress. Does this mean don't have extravagant ideas? Absolutely not. However, it is possible that there are small adjustments that can be made that lead to a bigger impact over time. I found this to be true while developing and operating Simple Positive Play. I support the idea that educational resources don't always have to include expensive supplies. Learning and growth can be difficult, but we should take opportunities to recognize the smaller successes we encounter and to problem-solve when we encounter struggles. The play component supports experimenting with ideas and resources to make them better. Simple, positive play is an intangible experience that incorporates design-thinking skills.

INSPIRE

There was a combination of experiences that inspired the creation of the organization Simple Positive Play. Part of it was visiting my hometown of Louisiana, Missouri, and wanting to contribute something positive. I was involved in several clubs and organizations to help the community during high school, and I wanted to continue that service as an adult. Another part was going through the Massive Open Online Course (MOOC) on New Librarianship with Professor R. David Lankes and questioning the concept of a library and a librarian. Does a library have to have a building? Can a librarian only connect people to information inside of a building? That course led to graduate school where I began with a short residency period that pushed me to use new technology and collaborate with people I had never met. Another driving factor was that I was getting frustrated in my role as a youth services specialist/librarian at work.

I've mentioned that the library I was working at was undergoing many changes when I was hired. In the beginning, I had a lot of freedom to add programs, including a biweekly story-time program for ages up to two years old and their families. I was working to fill in the gaps in programming for youth from birth to age seventeen. The centralized Youth Services Department was also working toward supporting all twenty branches by offering to schedule paid presenters, developing a system-wide series of programs, and utilizing the communications department to streamline and promote those events. System-wide collaborations continued to grow, and opportunities to host programs developed through those collaborations also increased.

I wanted to be involved in all of it. I felt that if I didn't offer to host all system-wide program offerings at my branch, I was doing the community I served a disservice. I still had access to use the Communications Department for my own programs, but I didn't want people in my community to not see their branch on the menu of locations for programs presented at several other locations. Although I was almost never discouraged from creating my own programs or consulting with my branch management team about my own ideas, I felt that if I didn't present what was being offered through the centralized Youth Services Department, I wasn't being a team player and supporting my organization to the fullest. On the other hand, I wanted to play with program structure and collaborate more with other branches. The structure was becoming stifling. Ultimately, I decided that I didn't necessarily have to use my job to explore my ideas. The structure is easier to change when it is small and even easier when you create it yourself.

Inspiration for the first event for Simple Positive Play came from the idea of lemonade stands. I had noticed in my search for neat program ideas that it was approaching National Lemonade Day. I was attempting to create my own collection of resources and was fascinated by the idea of makerspaces, so I combined the ideas to promote a "make your own" lemonade stand, where I did provide lemonade for others, but I also included recipes for those that came to the stand to make their own. I also paired the stand with several tables of art supplies for kids to explore. My parents' driveway in Louisiana, Missouri, was the perfect setting for this event.

EMPATHIZE

The empathizing phase includes learning more about the community you are trying to serve.[5] I already had a bit of a relationship with the community I was serving in Louisiana, Missouri, because it is where I grew up and where a good portion of my family and schoolmates still lived with their own children. The Louisiana Public Library hosted some programs for young people, but there wasn't a dedicated employee focused on youth services like I experienced working for a larger library system. My own experiences of being able to explore town influenced my desire to create a safe space to play and create.

There are more structured ways of understanding the community. The Design Thinking Toolkit provides methods for researching communities. They include user interviews, expert interviews, observations, immersive experiences, and analogous settings.[6] It is all about showing that you are willing to listen to the community and that you have a desire to help meet a community need. Although it may seem like you are just having a conversation, those conversations can be opportunities to ask questions about existing programs and services and what they might want to see in the future.

Paying attention to how participants interact in the existing environment can give you opportunities to notice when something could be presented in a better way. For example, I used to create beautiful little packs of crafts for story time. At one point, I placed the packs in front of each chair like I was setting a table for dinner. Kids would move the packs or grab someone else's pack or dump their pack onto the table in a way that resulted in most of the contents landing on the floor. I was putting in a lot of effort, but my methods needed to be adjusted. Instead of individual packs at individual stations, I started creating little craft charcuterie boards or collections that contained all the supplies and that all kids could access.

Having a young child of my own at the time, I went to different children's events and observed the way I felt as a parent at children's events. One influential experience for me was at the St. Louis Art Museum in St. Louis, Missouri. The St. Louis Art Museum is located in Forest Park and across the street from the St. Louis Zoo. All of these places have no admission costs, so it is a great place to enjoy multiple free quality attractions and the only cost concern for my family was driving there.

The St. Louis Art Museum hosted family days and would offer an art project and stroller tours. My child and I went to one of the family days and got one pack of supplies to create illuminated art projects from the front of the room and headed to our workspace. My kid is fairly independent when it comes to creating her own things, but I was uncomfortable when she started using the gold foil we received in a way that made me want to correct her. She wasn't hurting herself or anyone else, but I was so excited for her to have the chance to use gold foil and didn't want her to "waste" it. I finally approached the entrance table and asked if I could have a kit for myself. When I reflected on the event, I was thankful that I had the opportunity to work on a project alongside my child. My child seemed pleased that I stopped interrupting her process. From then on, we always grabbed a kit for each of us and chatted together while we worked on projects.

I've also been asked to leave a library program with my child when she was about three years old in another library system. I'll admit, my child doesn't always enter a room and sit quietly on the carpet. When we entered the room, she sat for a little while but then wanted to get up. We moved to the back of the room where she was attracted to the room partition screen. The general warning of "those who continue to make noise will be asked to leave and go to the children's area" was given. I will argue that it was not my kid that made the final noise that broke the camel's back, but the presenter stopped the program, looked at me, and asked us to leave. Everything in me wanted to say, "It wasn't my kid!" But I didn't. I picked up my kid, and we moved toward the children's area. On the way out, we were told we could come back later for the activity. When it came time for the activity, a library worker came to us and invited us back in. By that time, my kid was happy choosing books and playing with the puppets, and I was embarrassed. We didn't go back in.

This library experience influenced the way I implemented programs with young children. The library presenter at this particular program didn't do anything wrong that I can pinpoint and define. I can't say that I would have handled the situation differently. I just know that I didn't feel good about myself as a mother when I left the library that day. I showed up on time and my kid was within the age group advertised for the program. Was I too engaged with the program myself and not paying close enough attention to my child? Probably. My takeaway was thinking about how I would adjust the presentation of my own programs to make sure that new parents and families with young children felt engaged and comfortable.

The Design Thinking for Libraries Toolkit also includes other ways of researching the community that I like to think of as community icebreakers. The toolkit offers methods like card sorts, photo essays, and journey maps.[7] I have not employed any of these methods, but am intrigued by the idea of using hands-on experiences to learn more about the community.

The surveys conducted by Clarke et al. revealed that, out of the respondents who were familiar with design thinking, empathizing was the most familiar stage, and while understanding the community is extremely important, there are more skills within the design-thinking process that can be beneficial.[8]

DEFINE

The defining stage is the opportunity to focus and clearly identify what problem you want to solve and what resources you bring to finding the solution. The problem I was trying to solve by creating Simple Positive Play was largely personal. I wanted to give myself more opportunities to develop a service to see if the community would support it. One thing I had to consider was whether I would charge for my events. Although I love the idea of having more financial freedom, my goal was to help young people and their caregivers use their imagination to create whatever they wanted to create. Charging for my services would have put me in the position to say "no" to some of the people who could benefit from what I wanted to offer.

Defining what I wanted to accomplish was integral to this stage, too. The mission for Simple Positive Play is to facilitate playful experiences for young people and their families while promoting an engaged and informed community. I wanted to identify what my goals were so that the next stage of ideation and brainstorming would become more focused.

Developing the definition for what I wanted to accomplish took a lot of consideration. I had to consider the resources available to me to implement my idea. I did not have the same kind of budget or physical resources that I had available to me working for a large library system. I did have a personal collection of books I was willing to share, some personal budget, and access to a great local organization to purchase inexpensive material. Leftovers, Etc. is a business in the St. Louis region that stocks its shelves with things crafty people desperately want to remove from theirs. Things like yarn, fabric, art supplies, office supplies, building material, recyclable plastics, aluminum, and more. For the price of $7, I could fill a large paper bag with plenty of products for play. Additionally, if you were ever looking for a dozen empty two-liter bottles with lids, you could place an order and they'd pack it up for you and charge a per-item price.

At the library, a tool I would use to define my role was listed in my job description. It included the line about providing programs for ages birth through seventeen years old. Additional tasks included connecting with schools and community organizations, providing customer service, and completing statistics. I referred to my job description regularly to define the structure of my work environment. The mission statement of the library system was posted on my computer, and I had the opportunity to be involved with the development of the library's strategic plan. Knowing the goals of the organization and my role within the plan inspired me to be creative within that framework.

The Design Toolkit for Libraries provides tips for how to define the challenge.[9] It offers solutions for making sure your problem-solving goals aren't too broad or too narrow. It can be difficult to construct a goal that is "just right," but as much as it influences the stages to follow, the flexibility of the design-thinking process allows you to revisit the defining stage even after you've moved to a different stage in the process.

IDEATION AND BRAINSTORMING

The ideation phase is when you look at who you're working with, what you have to offer, what the problem is, and what you are going to do about it. This is when you start sharing your goals with those who are willing to work with you to solve the problem or challenge you've identified.

One of my favorite things to do when visiting my hometown is to go to the riverfront and check in on the Mississippi River. We are a floodplain, and I like looking at water levels and enjoying the scenery. One day, after hosting another event at my parent's driveway, I decided to walk through the downtown area located a few blocks away from the riverfront. I had been taking pictures on this trip and wanted to get some images of the historic architecture. I noticed a new art studio that I had never seen before. As I was checking out the whimsical, colorful artwork in the display window from across the street, a gentleman stepped out and invited me in, and that's when I met the artist, his wife, Kae Pea.

The name of the studio was called The Moon and the Maker and wasn't technically opened when her husband had invited me in. I loved the work that I saw throughout the studio, and we started a conversation. They were familiar with my family because they were involved with their kids in the school district, and their familiarity with the football team explained why they knew my uncle and a few of my cousins. When I shared that I had just invited kids to my parents' driveway to engage with art supplies, she shared that she had classroom space in the back that she was hoping to start hosting classes and workshops. She then offered to let me use the space once a month at no cost. She shared her expectations, such as making sure that children didn't run through the studio, and that took Simple Positive Play from the driveway to a studio.

By sharing our stories with one another, Kae Pea and I were able to develop a framework where we could work together to brainstorm a solution that I wanted to solve. It was a mutually beneficial collaboration because she wanted to provide more access to the classroom space and help adults explore their creativity and adults would be bringing their children to the space to engage in creative making activities. I was able to find an indoor space to connect families to playful resources.

This experience is a very simplified version of brainstorming a solution, but the Design Thinking for Libraries Toolkit[10] outlines ways to connect with other partners by telling and listening to stories to identify common themes. Sitting around listening to others tell stories can be an arduous task if participants begin to go on tangents or lose focus on the point of the story. The toolkit provides an approach that is engaging and focused.

After speaking with Kae Pea and her husband, we found that we both wanted to develop an environment where participants can be creative. The toolkit encourages you to develop a framework to illustrate the common theme.[11] The framework doesn't have to be overly complicated, and it is likely to change. This process is what the toolkit describes as one of the "most mentally exhausting part of the design thinking process."[12] Different approaches and exercises to help develop these frameworks are provided to guide the reader, and it can be as simple as creating a Venn diagram to show where efforts and interests overlap.

Brainstorming, for me, is far more entertaining than setting up frameworks. It is an opportunity to consider the resources I have and then let my imagination run wild. Brainstorming with others can have its own set of obstacles. Sometimes people don't share their ideas because they feel they are dumb or silly. As long as we're still brainstorming about the same general idea, brainstorming sessions are the perfect time to share big ideas and learn about the big ideas of others. Brainstorming provides the opportunity to combine ideas, which could inspire a different idea. I love imagining brainstorming sessions as a room full of people shooting ideas like non-lethal bolts of lightning and generating sparks that illuminate the space.

PROTOTYPING AND TESTING

Prototyping means creating a sample of the solution you developed through brainstorming. The first event for Simple Positive Play in my parents' driveway was, essentially, a prototype of what Simple Positive Play looks like today, but it wasn't the only time that idea of simple, positive play was developed on a smaller scale. I was able to host "make your own" sessions at The Moon and The Maker for about two years before the studio moved to a location that didn't have the same kind of space available for classes or sessions with younger children.

In 2015, Monica Wideman, a parent who lived near the library branch I worked at, reached out to share a project she wanted to explore. Her vision was to create an indoor play space for children that was located near her community in North St. Louis County. Although there are free attractions at Forest Park in St. Louis City, it is still at least a twenty-minute drive to access. Other free resources were located farther away and charge admission for access. I was invited to attend a meeting in her backyard to contribute ideas alongside other community members.

In this scenario, those at the meeting and I agreed that the organization to establish an indoor play space would operate under the name Simple Positive Play, and I made the decision to apply for our 501(c)(3) nonprofit status. While we waited to be approved, we had meetings with the Parks and Recreation of Florissant, Missouri, and came to an agreement to use a meeting space at Sunset Park for play.

We hosted an event that included a story time and a Kindermusik session along with snacks and open indoor play. For future play times, the park ranger would be on-site to help people sign in, and parents would move to the lower space to engage with the toys we set up in the space. It was a smaller space and didn't require us to have many toys to make the space seem full. We were not expected to be on location to help facilitate play. When we made the schedule, some play sessions occurred during the workday. I would spend my lunch break driving to the location to clean up and prepare for the next day.

Prototyping is a great way to experiment and finetune an idea before implementing it in a bigger way. The library can use the skill of prototyping to test out certain aspects of a program. I would use teen volunteers to help prototype programs for other teens and children. For one program, I wanted to combine a mini-golf kit with small, circular robots called Spheros that could be guided by using an app on an iPad. At first, I introduced the Sphero to the teen volunteers before I introduced the Sphero to the upper elementary aged participants in my program. After that, I combined the mini-golf kit and the Spheros with the teen volunteers before later implementing the program with upper-elementary-aged participants. The practice of prototyping with teens and taking into account their input helped me to troubleshoot problems during my program. It also helped me determine which parts of the mini-golf kit wouldn't be necessary for the actual program I implemented a few weeks later.

Iteration

The design-thinking process doesn't fit into a nice checklist where you can check off a particular item when you are finished. It involves constantly reflecting and assessing the various aspects of the program or service including the community needs, partners, and solutions. Sometimes an idea is developed through an observation or a problem needs to be redefined. At Simple Positive Play, every open-play session provides an opportunity to grow.

After working with the Florissant Parks and Recreation Department to test an indoor space for playful resources, we were able to start working with the Ferguson Parks and Recreation Department and eventually obtained a more permanent location at January-Wabash Park. We now had experience in setting up a play space and were able to create a schedule where a Simple Positive Play volunteer was able to help facilitate a playful experience for young people and their families.

Every open-play session provides an opportunity to make the experience better. Observing the way that children interact and engage with the material helps us decide on whether the material is needed and whether we need to get more resources for a particular feature like the light table or play kitchen. There is a kitchen area that houses our mini-makerspace, and it contains art supplies, craft projects, LEGOs, sensory toys, and toys that teach coding skills.

During play, we can have conversations with the young people and their adults and hear stories about the need for more opportunities to interact and play with other kids that aren't too far away from home. Feedback from early childhood educators inspired us to start transforming part of our storage into a space where participants can have a quieter space if they need it.

The Design Thinking for Libraries Toolkit provides many examples of how to understand and implement design thinking skills, and it requires time and practice to use them all effectively. I'm not declaring that I have used all of the skills in the best possible way, but I do believe that design-thinking skills are applicable to the work libraries do within the community.

The concept of simple, positive play reminds me to think big but to not overcomplicate solutions to problems. Otherwise, it is difficult to figure out the very first step toward a goal. The uncertainty I felt at work inspired me to create something outside of work, but I started small and simply to prototype and test the kind of space I wanted to help create. Even if a program or service doesn't go exactly to plan, it is okay to try again and to believe in the idea enough to persevere and pursue it again. For me, that idea was operating an organization that helps families connect with each other while also learning and having good experiences.

Simple, positive play can also be applied when facilitating STEM and creative projects in open-ended programs. When young people navigate design-thinking skills through these programs, kids can get frustrated or overwhelmed. It is helpful to help them navigate the project if you keep the initial stages simple and allow for them to iterate their ideas over the course of the program. If the first prototype doesn't work or look the way a participant wants it to look, it is okay. There isn't a grade, and they can try again.

NOTES

1. IDEO, *Design Thinking for Libraries: A Toolkit for User-centered Design*, 2015, http://designthinkingforlibraries.com/toolkit.

2. "What Is Design Thinking?" Interaction Design Foundation, accessed November 25, 2022, https://www.interaction-design.org/literature/topics/design-thinking#:~:text=Design%20thinking%20is%20an%20iterative%2C%20non%2Dlinear%20process%20which%20focuses,%2C%20Ideate%2C%20Prototype%20and%20Test.

3. Rachel Ivey Clarke, Ann Rosenblad, and Satyen Amonkar, "Design Thinking and Methods in Library Practice and Graduate Library Education," School of Information Studies-Faculty Scholarship, 2019, https://surface.syr.edu/istpub/190.

4. Clarke, Rosenblad, and Amonkar, "Design Thinking and Methods in Library Practice and Graduate Library Education," 24.

5. Rikke Friis Dam, "The 5 Stages in the Design-thinking Process," Interaction Design Foundation, accessed June 2022, https://www.interaction-design.org/literature/article/5-stages-in-the-design-thinking-process.

6. *Design Thinking for Libraries*, 34.

7. *Design Thinking for Libraries*, 35.

8. Clarke, Rosenblad, and Amonkar, "Design Thinking and Methods in Library Practice and Graduate Library Education," 24.

9. *Design Thinking for Libraries*, 30.

10. *Design Thinking for Libraries*, 51.

11. *Design Thinking for Libraries*, 57.

12. *Design Thinking for Libraries*, 57.

7

Collaboration

Collaborating with others on a larger project can be a rewarding experience. I've participated in theater productions from a young age. The entire process of meeting others through the audition, getting a role, rehearsing, and finally piecing it together for opening night produces a large range of emotions from the beginning to closing night. Everyone involved has a responsibility that contributes to the overall success of the production. Although I've had onstage roles, there have been many times when I wasn't the talent on stage but was behind the scenes making sure the environment was prepared, assisting actors and actresses with quick costume changes, operating the lighting and sound equipment, and coordinating quick set changes. My internship in college led me to work at a movie studio in New York City where I assisted the publicity, acquisitions, and legal departments as I tried to soak up as much information as I could in a semester away from home in a large city. I discovered that there are so many more people who bring a production together, and even the credits at the end of a movie don't necessarily include everyone who had a role in taking an idea and transforming it into a film that is, hopefully, enjoyed by people worldwide.

I can relate to the library as a production. Before working in a library, I knew that there were people who placed items on the shelves, and I was familiar with library workers providing assistance when it came to circulating material or understanding how to operate library equipment. In school and in my hometown library, it was all the same person. It was not until I worked in a large library system that I began to comprehend or even think about the many different areas of expertise that coalesce to create a functioning library. I've been a part of a one-woman show and I've been in larger productions, and in every circumstance, it has been the collaboration of people with many talents working together to share a product with the community. Everyone has a role in making a product and, although the library isn't selling a tangible product, it is promoting learning and knowledge creation. Working effectively with others, within the library and with other organizations who share similar interests, can contribute to continuously developing innovative services as information and community needs change.

Patricia Montiel-Overall wrote a paper called "Toward a Theory of Collaboration for Teachers and Librarians"[1] that examines the definition of collaboration and identifies four models of working together for a common goal. The four models include coordination, cooperation/partnerships, integrated instruction, and integrated curriculum, and the key characteristics that differentiate each model are the varying degrees of intent, intensity, and interest. Although this paper focuses on the relationship between teachers and school library media specialists, it provides a great amount of insight for public youth services specialists and librarians wanting to collaborate with an organization that shares a similar audience.

Montiel-Overall begins with what she refers to as Model A or coordination.[2] In this stage, the effort is minimal and includes scheduling time to assist with an activity or making sure the library is available to use for a project or event. There is a relationship that grows out of this sort of activity, but coordination usually manifests as one person taking the lead and directing the communication among participants.

Coordination takes place quite a bit when scheduling outreach to schools to promote the Summer Reading Club program through the library system. Each year the Youth Services Department at the main, centralized library or headquarters location would send out communication to a list of schools and childcare facilities in the library system's service area. The letter or email would promote the benefits of the Summer Reading Club program and offer the prospect of a youth services specialist or librarian to present the program to the students. I, as a youth librarian, would follow up to discuss potential styles of a presentation, whether it be traveling from classroom to classroom to speak for ten minutes, spending a day in the library as classrooms rotate through, presenting to a gymnasium full of students, or providing a story time along with information about Summer Reading Club. The librarian would then coordinate with the teachers and find a day that works best, and I'd show up, present the information in the designated space (or spaces), and then leave. Much of the coordination was performed by the school media specialist or librarian. I essentially provided a menu of options, and when I was available, the school media specialist/librarian either accepted the offer for a presentation or declined.

Visiting schools in person to share information not only helped me to start a working relationship with the school media specialist/librarian, but it also allowed me to start building a relationship with the students. I would often see students who came to library programs in the audience of a presentation. Sometimes students who still came to the library but didn't go to programs would notice me on a later visit to the library, and I was a familiar face to help the navigate the collection.

In one situation, the school media specialist/librarian wanted to provide the opportunity for students to learn about the Summer Reading Club program and ask questions, but none of the format options were feasible. However, the school media specialist/librarian stayed intent on getting Summer Reading Club program information to students and offered to record my presentation to then send to teachers to view in their classroom when it was most convenient. This was a creative way to disseminate information, and although it took away the opportunity for me to engage with more students and teachers, it satisfied the goal of sharing information with students.

Montiel-Overall describes the cooperation/partnerships model, or Model B, as an approach to co-plan an end product.[3] School library media specialists and librarians are an ideal partner for public youth librarians since they are in a position to reach and interact with the audience we want to attract to the library. Additionally, the information literacy and problem-solving skills students practice within the library and at library programs can be useful in a school setting. The task of understanding the dynamics of each school or organization whose goals align with the library can be daunting when you have to cultivate relationships within different frameworks.

The relationship between the library branch I worked at and the schools in my area were a little complicated. The service area for my library included schools and childcare facilities within a physical boundary. This boundary encompassed almost two dozen daycares, private schools, and schools within two large public school districts. As a county library system, the physical space of my boundary included schools only located in areas served by the St. Louis County government. However, there are several municipalities within the county who have their own government and public libraries to provide resources and information needs. As far as access to library resources is concerned, the library systems in the St. Louis area have collaborated so that people who reside in other communities in the area, whether St. Louis City, St. Louis County, municipalities, or even neighboring St. Charles county, can get a free library card for any of those libraries and have more access to different collections.

Trying to enter the framework of entire school districts provided some challenges. I was invited to share information about our library resources and introduce myself as a community partner. During this meeting, I spoke about some of the resources available, like book discussion kits, databases, and our annual Summer Reading Club program. I shared my willingness to present library information to students and demonstrated ways to navigate the library website and catalog. There was one particular librarian who was, very noticeably, not interested in anything I was saying. Her arms and legs were crossed, and her body was shifted in her seat to turn away from me. It appeared as though she was one step away from completely turning her chair around to face the back wall. I had never met this person before. During this meeting, I wanted to learn more about what I could do or provide to help the library workers of the district share helpful resources with the families they serve so I started a conversation. The individual who was turned away mentioned that her students live in the municipality and that what I was sharing didn't apply to her or her students. In some ways, I could understand her viewpoint.

Previous to this meeting, I had been actively pursuing partnerships with schools within my physical service area, but that excluded those schools located within the municipality, as well as other schools located in the county but served by a different county library youth services specialist. By the time this meeting occurred, it could be perceived that I was only interested in speaking to part of the team and dismissing other communities within the district. At this meeting, I compiled a list of all the schools within the school district and paired them with the public library closest to their community. Even though the entire school district spanned across the service area of a couple of county library branches, there were also schools located within the municipality. I had also prepared for this meeting by inviting my colleagues within the county library system to join the meeting and connecting with the youth librarian at the municipality to ask what information I could share to promote their services.

My goal of this meeting wasn't to exclude anyone. It was a prime opportunity to reinforce and start building relationships between public libraries and the school district. It was an attempt to start designing a partnership that was mutually beneficial and through that one person's body language and following conversations, I could identify obstacles.

This meeting helped me to come to terms with my own limitations in trying to promote library services. I'm thankful for the librarians who shared their wisdom and insight. They were mentors to me as I hadn't yet gone to graduate school for library science, and they had worked in the school system for multiple years. These librarians would come to the public library after school, and we'd have more conversations about what a successful collaboration could look like. They started including me in conversations about school-specific programs and events, and we ultimately designed unique experiences for families in the community.

We were able to host family nights at the library for one elementary school. The librarian had the idea of inviting families to the library for stories, activities, and a library tour. We coordinated our roles and co-presented at the event. This type of an event is an example of Model B because, although we agreed on the different roles we would play during this event, we worked independently on our roles and shared presentation time.

Model C is known as integrated instruction. In a school setting, the school media specialist/librarian and the instructor co-design the experience with a shared objective in mind.[4] In this model, there is an increased level of responsibility to bring your own individual expertise to the situation and design a more cohesive experience for students to learn. The experience would include a balanced amount of information literacy and curriculum instruction.

Collaboration between a school library media specialist/librarian and a youth services specialist/librarian would also include sharing responsibilities and a balanced approach. While trying to build relationships with the schools in my service area, I met a high school librarian who was very successful with connecting teens to library resources. During every lunch period, the library was full of students, and she hosted many after school clubs, including the Student Library Advisory Council (SLAC), whose participating members proudly called themselves SLACkers. This group participated in reading incentive programs and were rewarded with things like read-a-thons, where they were granted permission to socialize, read outside, and eat pizza in lieu of going to class.

This librarian, Ms. Buckley, had a strong relationship with her students and she allowed me to come in so that she could introduce me to more teens in the community. The more often I came in to share current events happening at the public library, the more opportunities we had to talk to one another and share potential ways to work together. One of the needs she noticed in her library was that there were several students who either had younger siblings or who had children themselves. She decided that she would establish a children's library within the school library space to provide more resources for students who didn't necessarily have transportation to go to the public library. Some of her students expressed interest in being able to read stories and provide craft activities for preschool-aged children. Story times were one of the only programs that I had implemented on a weekly basis. We worked together to design a story time that was presented after school. The high school was also the site for an early childhood education classroom for preschool-aged children. Although the teens were out of school, the early childhood education classroom still had another hour to the day. Through trial and error, we developed a program that included preschool children, teens, a public librarian, a high school librarian, and early childhood educators. It required more effort to establish versus just coming in to talk about programs, but it helped teens become more involved at the library and some started to volunteer at the public library.

The final model in Montiel-Overall's efforts to develop a theory about collaboration is Model D, or integrated curriculum. Integrated curriculum includes the ability to not just collaborate with one teacher but also to collaborate with all curriculum in all grade levels.[5] Out of all of the models, this is the only one to account for the role that a principal plays in providing the space for and expectation of collaboration in order to enhance the student learning experience on a larger scale.

Applying the integrated curriculum model to the collaborations created with youth services specialists/librarians and any other organization would not look the same as it does in a school since public library youth services specialists don't necessarily align with a curriculum. Even within each school or school district, the details on the way the collaborations form can look different. However, the characteristics that are a part of developing a collaboration is the overall goal and the amount of time and energy spent developing problem-solving solutions either between departments or organizations.

The library system I had worked for was involved in collaborations and partnerships with multiple different organizations, so in addition to working toward connecting with other teachers and schools in my service area, I also had a role in the collaboration the library developed with other community organizations. For instance, leadership within the library system connected with area hospitals for a program for new parents, food banks to provide summer lunches, and restaurants and sports teams to add to our summer reading club program. There was an outreach department that focused on bookmobile services, but, even though these collaborations served schools and students within my service area, my role was minimal or non-existent. Although the arrangements made with outside organizations provided an introduction or conversation starters about services the library had to offer, collaborations and partnerships at an institutional level with schools, it didn't always present the opportunity to customize engagement with the community I served.

In the example I provided for Model A, my role as a youth services specialist/librarian was to speak to students about summer reading club, and it took time to coordinate but not as much time as it took to establish a relationship and work together to design the afterschool program with the high school librarian, early childhood educators, and teens. Considering the number of potential schools in my service area to collaborate with, having these larger efforts to connect people to resources was beneficial because I, as just one individual, could not possibly take the time to build relationships with each school and all of their teachers. However, when given the opportunity to build stronger relationships, I developed a greater understanding of challenges facing educators and was more capable of connecting information to information needs. I, personally, had more buy-in to my organization and was more motivated to provide feedback to enhance or alter library offerings to better address challenges facing the community. Collaboration at an institutional level and at a branch level helped to integrate the various resources I had available to me and helped me to have a stronger understanding of the library institution as a whole.

There isn't an institution quite like a public library, and recognizing the uniqueness of it helps to promote services and gather buy-in from the community. Nowhere else can a kid get a library card to have free access to products including books, movies, music, video games, and more. There is a sense of independence because there isn't always a homework assignment associated with the material they can choose to engage with, and their use of material isn't graded to determine what they can have access to next. As a youth services specialist/librarian, I get the opportunity to build relationships and invite young people to collaborate and become more invested in the types of resources the library can make available. Instead of just choosing from a menu of options, collaborations help participants design the menu and add their own expertise to the conversation. In the last collaboration, we went through the design-thinking process by defining the problem we wanted to solve and our role within our own individual frameworks and then working toward discovering a solution in which each of us could contribute to a potential solution. The experience in collaborating and partnering with students allows them to have a voice in their community.

Simply telling someone to collaborate with their community can be overwhelming to a person. Using the idea of a theater production as an example, if you are given a script and told to just make the production happen, it is hard to know where to start. Yes, you want to learn the story of the production and vaguely understand the different components that will need to come together, but one of the first things to determine is your own individual role that you are responsible for and how that role fits into the project. For instance, the onstage talent wants to determine how their character fits within the overall storyline just as much as the light board operator needs to determine how the design and use of lights can add depth and complexity to a moment on stage. Reviewing the core values of librarianship can assist with understanding just how the library, and, more specifically, individual librarians, fit into collaborative settings.

The American Library Association has identified several core values that help to define the role of a librarian whether in a public, school, academic, or special library system.[6] I've selected a few to discuss further as a way of helping librarians, future librarians, and those who work with librarians understand the expertise a librarian can potentially provide in a collaborative setting inside and outside of a library building. The core values that I will focus on fall into the categories of access, democracy, and professionalism, but other core values are integrated as it is sometimes difficult to separate them from one another. They all support and define the capabilities of a librarian.

One of the first things that people tend to think of when talking about a library is books. Some expect an individual library collection to have every book published on every topic available on the shelves, no matter the condition of the material. This is, of course, an exaggeration, but I've encountered dissatisfied and concerned patrons who disagree with the removal of children's book titles that are damaged or no longer in print. However, there is usually still an opportunity to have access to the title through other nearby library collections or the interlibrary loan service, but the title may no longer be as easily accessible as it had in the past. Beyond books, the library provides access to the internet and subscribes to databases allowing patrons to connect to job and educational opportunities in addition to entertainment like social media, movies, magazines, and music. Some library systems also provided access to resources for families like science kits, art supplies, and technology equipment. Access to this community collection isn't contingent on purchasing anything, and it provides a value.

The organization of Simple Positive Play focuses on providing access to playful resources. It is located between a county and a municipal library location, so, although there are books as part of the collection, the pressure or necessity to have every book ever published accessible within the space isn't a priority. Instead, the collection at Simple Positive Play is a combination of community donations and books selected for their artistic quality or connection to the community. The other resources like toys, art supplies, and the space itself provide families that don't have the space within their own home or the disposable income to experiment with toys at different stages of their children's development access to experiences not otherwise accessible to them.

A combination of the COVID-19 pandemic and the teacher shortage has created a situation for some families in which their child hasn't had much social engagement with their peers and they are on a waitlist to enter a classroom that can provide a positive learning experience. Providing free access to these types of resources for caregivers to use with their children helps to bridge gaps in development. Collaborating with parents and early childhood educators has helped to identify needs that can be addressed through cultivating a collection and service that promotes play and peer interaction.

The core value of democracy highlights the autonomous nature of a library. Libraries support freedom of speech in a variety of formats, which also leads to inviting patrons to help shape the library in their community. Libraries are expected to value the input from community members in order to create and design the collection and services the library provides. As an adult, I am expected to vote in elections and share feedback that can influence laws and policies. For young people, they don't always have the opportunity to have their voices and ideas heard and acted upon. Collaborating with young people gives them the experience to share their opinion and contribute to a service that affects them. As a youth librarian, I get to help share and amplify their voice in situations where they can't do it themselves.

The core value of professionalism supports the "provisions of library services by professionally qualified personnel who have been educated in graduate programs within institutions of higher education."[7] I do not believe that only people with a master's degree in library and information science are capable of being able to collaborate. However, those with an advanced degree should have a greater understanding of the dynamics of a library system and act as a leader in professional situations. Being a leader doesn't necessarily mean being in charge of everyone at the table but rather asking questions and supporting the conversation with experience, background knowledge, and an eagerness to listen to others in order to focus efforts to implement or share an idea.

The book *Collective Genius: The Art and Practice of Leading Innovation* by Linda A. Hill, Greg Barbandeau, Emily Truelove, and Kent Lineback developed the term "collective genius" to explain the way the leaders of innovative companies like Pixar continue to develop successful projects. Collective genius is when "every person in your group, whether that's a small team or a large corporation, contains a slice of genius." The leader's responsibility is to "create a place where all of those slices can be elicited, combined and converted into collective genius."[8] This term can also apply to the way leadership in the library has the potential to develop collections, services, and partnerships that are beneficial for and utilized by the community.

The book discusses the challenges of working with a group of creative individuals that contribute to the products of an organization and how the path to reach a new product or service is not always a step-by-step process that moves in a forward direction. Identifying different stages in the development process provides a structure, but the work within that structure can seem chaotic as progress sometimes means revisiting different decisions made early on in the project or encountering situations in which a previous plan was no longer going to be deemed successful. In an organization like Pixar that experiments to innovate, a strictly trial-and-error approach can cost a significant amount of time and money. However, if properly led, the different talents of the team can be "harnessed" to allow for creative exploration while also staying on task.[9]

The researchers observed several different leaders of successful industries and found that the leaders all had a few things in common. Each leader was able to "collaborate, learn through discovery learning and make integrative decisions."[10] The environment created for individuals to collaborate with each other encouraged conversation, feedback, and the critical assessment of ideas. The library, as a locally accessible institution embedded in communities all over the country, can serve as an environment for innovation not just for community members but for the institution itself. As such, all library workers should be led to consider themselves as experts in their position and leaders when they represent the library in collaborative endeavors with their community. This doesn't necessarily mean being in charge of every project but recognizing that each individual's experience can add a perspective to the conversation that contributes to the success of the organization.

There is no way that the organization of Simple Positive Play could have continued to exist and grow if it wasn't for the input of other leaders within the community. The parent who first approached me about developing Simple Positive Play in the north St. Louis County area had strengths that lied within her community relationships and human resources experience. She was also very active in taking her children to different child and family-friendly attractions throughout the region. Although I had taken my child to some of the attractions, this parent was far more knowledgeable about their locations and costs, which led her to identify a need for more playful spaces closer to her neighborhood. Thankfully, leaders of the Parks and Recreation Department were willing to listen to and empathize with the goals of Simple Positive Play. All of this led to a presentation and conversations with members of the Ferguson City Council, who allowed us to use space within the community to bring more playful experiences to families in the area. These collaborations required an immense amount of time and effort to develop trust and a deeper understanding of the roles each person would play in making Simple Positive Play possible. Collaboration is an ongoing process both in developing the collection and services provided by Simple Positive Play and in working with young people as they navigate new experiences.

Another way to think about collaboration is through the concept of simple, positive play. Collaborations don't have to start off as being a massive undertaking with hundreds or dozens of people to organize and focus efforts. It can start off with an idea that pulls together the talents and experiences of a few people who experiment, or play, with the idea and then invite others, like other organizations, corporations, colleagues, or young people, to join the effort.

NOTES

1. Patricia Montiel-Overall, "Toward a Theory of Collaboration for Teachers and Librarians," *School Library Media Research* 8 (2005): 8. https://www.ala.org/aasl/sites/ala.org.aasl/files/content/aaslpubsandjournals/slr/vol8/SLMR_Theoryof-Collaboration_V8.pdf.
2. Montiel-Overall, "Toward a Theory of Collaboration," 10.
3. Montiel-Overall, "Toward a Theory of Collaboration," 12.
4. Montiel-Overall, "Toward a Theory of Collaboration," 14.
5. Montiel-Overall, "Toward a Theory of Collaboration," 16–17.
6. "Core Values of Librarianship," American Library Association, July 26, 2006, https://www.ala.org/advocacy/intfreedom/corevalues.
7. "Core Values of Librarianship," American Library Association.
8. Linda A. Hill, Greg Barbandeau, Emily Truelove, and Kent Lineback, *Collective Genius: The Art and Practice of Leading Innovation*, (Boston, MA: Harvard Business Review Press, 2014), Introduction, Kindle.
9. Hill et al., *Collective Genius*, chap. 1, Kindle.
10. Hill et al., *Collective Genius*, chap. 1, Kindle.

8

Playwork

Comparing a library to a playground seems dangerous. No, I am not advocating for children to be climbing on the shelves or jumping off of the furniture, but I do want children to know that they have many permissions to access the resources we have available for them. The Oxford Dictionary of English gives one definition of a playground as "an outdoor area provided for children to play in, especially at a school or public park." The alternate definition is "a place where a particular group of people choose to enjoy themselves."[1] The first definition encompasses what a person might envision when hearing the word "playground," especially when discussing topics like play and young people. However, the atmosphere of a library where children feel welcome to enjoy access to information and resources fits the definition of playground, too.

Children don't always enter a playground knowing how each individual piece of equipment works, but, with some guidance, they figure out how to climb the ladder to eventually go down the slide. They may need a push in the swing, but many eventually learn how to reach incredible heights using the swinging motion of their own body. Some kids go to the playground and have to explore every single square inch, while others are content with climbing the same piece of equipment over and over again in new and different ways.

My influence for this comparison comes from the physical playground being part of my independent exploration of my hometown. My walks to the library always included a stop to get snacks and a trip to the playground. However, the whole experience was an adventure. There were dangerous obstacles like crossing the road. I even had to use some problem-solving skills in order to figure out the most effective use of the small amount of money in my pocket. Before being old enough to walk the journey by myself, my older sister would escort me. Later, I would take my younger sisters sometimes, which made it a different kind of adventure for me.

ADVENTURE PLAYGROUNDS

The first iteration of an adventure playground was developed by C. T. Sorenson in the 1930s in Denmark.[2] Sorenson noticed that children preferred to play with random, spare materials instead of using the playground equipment he supplied for them. From this observation, the idea of a "junk playground" was realized. Lady Allen of Hurtwood took the concept of an "adventure playground" to London, and it has expanded from there.

In a video produced by Stanley Shofield productions and presented by the National Playing Fields Association,[3] viewers are shown an adventure playground in action. The location for the adventure playground in the video is a bomb site from World War II and suggests using the corner of an existing playground or a plot of land that will be soon be developed. Narrator John Snagge describes the playground and shares more detail about how adventure playgrounds operate. One of the features that make an adventure playground successful include the presence and support of play leaders. This video shows children doing some potentially dangerous things like building fires, playing battle games, and using hammers and nails to create forts. All of this play is supervised, but effective play leaders don't interfere with the space as much as they support the ideas of the participants using the space.

The National Play Fields Association collaborated with the play advocate organizations PLAYLINK and the Children's Play Council to develop the publication "Best Play: What Play Provisions Should Do for Children."[4] "Best Play" serves as a guide and resource tool to equip those who provide playful experiences for young people, also known as "playworkers," with information regarding the meaning of play and how play influences children's lives. The values and principles established by playworkers support many of the competencies for librarian services to children created by the Association for Library Services to Children (ALSC), which is a division of the American Library Association.

The ALSC competencies are grouped into different categories such as Collection Development and Management, Outreach and Advocacy, Administrative and Management Skills, and Professionalism and Professional Development, to name a few.[5] While characteristics from the previously mentioned categories are always present in some capacity in an organization like a library or nonprofit, the principles of playwork highly support the other three competency categories of Commitment to Client Group, Reference and User Services, and Programming Skills.

COMMITMENT TO CLIENT GROUP

The playwork principle of including children's views is mentioned as part of the Commitment to Client Group category. While one of the standards of this competency promotes children's librarians who "assess and respond on a regular and systematic basis to the needs and preferences of children, caregivers and educators that use the resources in the children's department, including those unserved and underserved by the library,"[6] playwork emphasizes the active inclusion of children and elevating the child's voice.[7] The playwork principle of respect for children also falls under the category of Commitment to Client group since playworkers and library workers both value the child as an individual.

The first standard listed under Commitment to Client also shows that playworkers and library workers are similar as it describes the need to respect the culturally diverse communities we work within. Other standards stress the importance of recognizing the struggles and obstacles that face the individual community members we serve. The playwork principle of equal entitlement complements the need to develop a space that is inclusive to ability and respectful of participants with varying backgrounds.

Another playwork principle is the recognition of children's abilities.[8] Play is something that children can participate in independently without much adult help. Similar to incorporating the children's voices in planning the space and programming, children are capable and welcome to navigate the library responsibly. This aligns with the Commitment to Client Group standard that encourages all youth library workers to have an understanding of learning theories related to infants, children, and adolescents. When interacting with older children, this is helpful to keep in mind because they are capable of searching for items in the catalog and finding books in numerical or alphabetical order. When working with younger children, this manifests as knowing toddlers aren't fans of sitting down and that story times must be dynamic in order to capture their attention.

There's a push-and-pull effect when it comes to recognizing a child's ability and providing the opportunity for growth. On one hand, there's a desire to cut out every piece of a story time craft for the child to glue to a picture. On the other hand, the story time craft also presents the opportunity for the participant to use scissors. There are several things that could go wrong with letting kids use scissors. What if they don't cut on the line? What if they cut their hair?

What if they cut someone else's hair? As a caregiver, playworker, or library worker, we're there to help educate the participant about how to use tools safely and how learning a new skill takes time and practice. These opportunities for growth don't present themselves if we don't recognize the importance of risk.[9]

Risk in an adventure playground looks like climbing to high places or using tools to build a shelter. In the library, a risk might include using a new tool or a new resource. In other words, it is trying something new. In a library, the risks are relatively low. As library workers, by teaching children how to look for books and boosting their confidence when it comes to finding information successfully, we're committed to empowering young people.

The last standard listed in the Commitment to Client Group category focuses on "removing barriers" as a public youth librarian.[10] This standard also resembles the playwork principle of providing access to rich, stimulating environments.[11] "Best Play" continues to describe creating a safe, playful, accessible space for children to engage with an array of resources.

The qualities of a youth services librarian and playworkers are very similar. Both groups create safe, enticing environments that allow children to become integrated into the community. Instead of doing things for young people, both groups work to participate with children to provide the kind of guidance and safety that helps them explore and grow in so many ways.

REFERENCE AND USER SERVICES

Children, caregivers, and educators don't always need our help when they enter the library. In fact, in some places, the use of self-checkout machines or a holds box that is accessible twenty-four hours a day nearly eliminates any opportunity for in-person engagement. However, when patrons do need our help, we want to be prepared. In playwork, it is very similar. A child can be given a cardboard box and they might climb inside or put it on their head. Some may sit on it or start putting other things inside. An adult in that situation might notice that the child is using their imagination to turn the box into a house. The adult can offer to cut or supervise the cutting of a door in the box to start making the house more of a reality. Engaged adults help to enhance a child's learning experience.

Playwork encourages "play for its own sake."[12] The library encourages reading, creating, and exploring for their own sake. This means that there isn't an expectation of a finished product after every interaction. In school, there are certain expectations that must be met. There isn't always time or material to let children explore and make mistakes.

There are times when kids seem to be overwhelmed by the choices that are available to them in a library or a play space like Simple Positive Play. A knowledgeable adult who helps to guide the patron more toward their wants and goals using readers' advisory and customer service skills can help a young person feel supported in their quest.

My favorite standard for the Reference and User Services category for youth librarians in a public library is the ability to "respect the patron's right to browse regardless of age and provides nonjudgemental answers to patron questions."[13] What if a young person comes in and has no idea where to start looking for an item they want? What if they don't even know what they want? The "freedom to browse" ultimately means developing a space where people feel like they belong. Providing freedom and belonging is shared with the playwork principle of providing young people the freedom to play.

Some children, caregivers, and educators have more obstacles in their daily lives than others. Providing a space where they aren't being judged for the questions or creative choices they face in their everyday lives can be like a deep breath. When you enter a library, there isn't an expectation of achievement or criticism, and that takes away some of the pressure we might feel when we're being evaluated.

PROGRAMMING SKILLS

Programming at a library adds an opportunity to build relationships with children, caregivers, and educators and provides engagement that can lead to feedback about services and other programs. There are characteristics from some of the other competencies that make programming more efficient. Being familiar with child development and child abilities helps to ensure that a program or activity isn't too hard or too easy for the majority of participants. Programming is a great way to showcase certain aspects of the collection and how to access them.

As much as the library collection is a physical space of accessible resources, the environment created for programming should be treated with care and attention to detail. The competency standard for programming skills includes recognizing the need for an environment that is also accessible and appropriate for the participants.[14] The playwork principle that is similar promotes access to stimulating environments.

"Best Play" acknowledges that there are times when an experience like a story or an activity can stir up some big emotions in young people. As a playworker, a principle to consider is being responsive to the child's needs.[15] In a library program, although it is important to be aware of the effect a program can potentially have on participants, it is difficult to address the emotional needs of a child who is feeling distraught. One of the standards in the Programming Skills competency pays attention to the importance of the parent or caregiver.[16] Parents are in the best position to assist a child when they have questions about sensitive topics or if a particular story unveils a strong emotion. Creating family programs where the parent-child relationship is supported and encouraged allows the chance for that relationship to strengthen as they learn how to navigate a program together.

Throughout this book, I've compared the work of youth public librarians to school librarians, teachers, and designers at Pixar. Through this chapter, I've compared the work of playworkers to that of the public youth librarian. I want to express that I am not trying to argue that youth librarians are to become replacements for the school environment or corporate-minded salespeople. Nor should we abandon the other competencies like collection management and professional development to play in a happy building and focus on teaching kids how to use scissors. Public library youth workers have a very dynamic role in facilitating programs in addition to helping library patrons navigate the resources available in the youth collection. Although there is some control over the information being presented in programs, the assistance provided when a caregiver or young person approaches the desk can vary widely. In some circumstances, we don't even interact with the patron in-person at all, but the patron experiences the environment that we've developed, welcoming them to utilize and play with the resources we're able to provide.

The concept of simple, positive play, from the point of view of someone operating an organization that focuses on young people and their families, means breaking down obstacles to accessing information and resources and innovating solutions. For parents and caregivers, it is an approach to assisting with their children's educational experiences by recognizing the resources already available within the household and the neighborhood. People don't have to complete any prerequisite courses to participate in simple, positive play. It's mainly about supporting the child's interest as they learn about the world around them. Youth public librarians are a major asset as they provide helpful guidance to children, caregivers, and educators as they experiment and play with information. The principles of playwork are very similar to some of the competencies for youth librarians and help us focus on connecting individuals to information.

NOTES

1. "Playground," in *Oxford Dictionary of English,* edited by Stevenson, Angus. Oxford University Press, 2010, https://www-oxfordreference-com.slcl.idm.oclc.org/view/10.1093/acref/9780199571123.001.0001/m_en_gb0639510. Reproduced with permission of the Licensor through PLSclear.

2. "Adventure Playground History," Rooted in Play, accessed November 25, 2022, https://www.rootedinplay.org/adventureplaygrounds#.

3. "Adventure Playground: Children Find Fun and Social Structure in World War 2 Bomb Site Rubble," YouTube Video, 13:52, https://www.youtube.com/watch?v=Uwj1wh5k5PY&t=2s.

4. National Playing Fields, *Best Play: What Play Provisions Should Do for Children*, (London: National Playing Fields Association, 2000). http://www.freeplaynetwork.org.uk/pubs/bestplay.pdf.

5. Association for Library Services to Children, "Competencies for Librarians Serving Children in Public Libraries," American Library Association, November 30, 1999. https://www.ala.org/alsc/edcareeers/alsccorecomps.

6. Association for Library Services to Children, "Competencies for Librarians Service Children in Public Libraries."

7. National Playing Fields, *Best Play*, 7.

8. National Playing Fields, *Best Play*, 8.

9. National Playing Fields, *Best Play*, 8.

10. Association for Library Services to Children, "Competencies for Librarians Service Children in Public Libraries."

11. National Playing Fields, *Best Play*, 7.

12. National Playing Fields, *Best Play*, 8.

13. Association for Library Services to Children, "Competencies for Librarians Serving Children in Public Libraries."

14. Association for Library Services to Children, "Competencies for Librarians Service Children in Public Libraries."

15. National Playing Fields, *Best Play,* 8.

16. Association for Library Services to Children, "Competencies for Librarians Service Children in Public Libraries."

9

The Importance of Stakeholders

Without the continued help of those who volunteered their time and talent, Simple Positive Play would look very differently than it does now. Without the support of stakeholders, it is hard to know if Simple Positive Play would exist at all. Understanding the stakeholders of the organization helps put all your effort into perspective.

Simple Positive Play is a completely volunteer-run organization. At this time, no one is being compensated for operating Simple Positive Play, and we are supported solely on donations from individuals and through family foundations. The City of Ferguson allows us to borrow space that used to house the Parks and Recreation office. They helped prep the space for us by clearing out old office furniture, painting the walls, and coordinating the replacement of the carpet, which was funded by an anonymous donor. The city even replaced a window that was broken during the civil unrest that occurred in Ferguson after the killing of Michael Brown in 2014. The Parks and Recreation Department works closely with us to make sure the space is safe and comfortable by shoveling snow in the parking lot, changing broken fluorescent bulbs, and fixing the air conditioning unit, when needed. The building that Simple Positive Play uses in Ferguson is located in a park where spiders can potentially find their way inside. The Parks and Recreation Department coordinates the extermination of spiders that would otherwise make the space unsafe for visitors.

Everyday Advocacy, a division of the Association for Library Services to Children (ALSC)[1] differentiates between primary and secondary stakeholders. Primary stakeholders are those that directly benefit from the services provided. For the youth library worker, this includes children of all ages, parents, educators, and organizations serving youth. These are people we connect with on a regular basis whether they frequently utilize library services or assist us with reaching young people to inform them about the services available with the organization.

Secondary stakeholders consist of those who are not necessarily coming into the library to use services or resources for young people but who recognize the importance of information literacy and support the efforts of the library to engage young people. These secondary supporters can include local businesses, government entities, philanthropists, and library support groups.

The identification of stakeholders may seem a little obvious. However, being more detailed with who the stakeholders of the organization actually are can lead to more specific ways that the library can identify and meet their information needs. Megan Oakleaf has done extensive research regarding assessing library services and providing impact in an academic library setting. She authored a workbook titled *Academic Library Value: The Impact Starter Kit*.[2] The workbook includes multiple exercises to guide librarians through the thought process of customizing an assessment of the services provided.

The Impact Starter Kit is flexible in that users of the book can complete every activity from start to finish or customize their navigation based on their own current needs and interests. The activities are broken down by headings like "First Things First," "Listening to Stakeholders," "Planning for Action," "Focusing on Impact," and more. The flexibility of this format enables users to focus on a particular theme. Each activity, in addition to being listed under a specific heading, is also identified by one of four themes: Rethinking, Listening, Getting Organized, and Taking Action.

The first step in the design-thinking process is to empathize or develop a deeper understanding of the population you are trying to serve. *The Impact Starter Kit* has a list of activities under the heading "Listening to Stakeholders," which stimulates more precise thinking about the population beyond looking at census data. It is a tool that can be useful in building and strengthening relationships that will be instrumental in inviting library users to become participants when developing library space, collection, programs, and services.

The "Institutional Focus Areas"[3] activity includes a checklist to help users identify the main focuses of the various stakeholders and directs users to add any that may be missing. Since this kit is designed to be used for academic libraries, the items listed on the checklist offer a general list of focuses to consider from the focus of students, faculty, institution, and community.

My experience using this kit comes from an assignment in graduate school where I partnered with public high school librarian, Ms. Rebecca Buckley, at McCluer High School in Ferguson, Missouri, to complete many of the activities to develop a final project synthesizing the information. Ms. Buckley had many years of experience working at McCluer High School and was one of the first librarians who I was able to start collaborating with as a youth services specialist at the nearby public library. She was very open to essentially partner with me for a semester. I am thankful that our working relationship was already established before embarking on this project, because it made the process more comfortable to execute.

The potential focuses listed under students in the "Institutional Focus Areas" activity didn't require a lot of adaptation to apply for high school students versus college students. The items include things concerning achievement, retention, and relationships. The possible focuses under the remaining headings of Faculty, Institution, and Community aren't unlike the same focuses a public high school librarian might support, but things like institutional branding, prestige, and affordability aren't necessarily in the top five focuses for a public high school librarian, which is what the activity instructs users to select. Users are instructed to then rank those top-five focuses and complete the T^3 process using the worksheet included for each activity.

The T^3 stands for Think, Talk, and Target and serves as a guided reflection after every activity and consists of the exact same after each activity. The Think portion provides opportunities to document thoughts, questions, and ideas generated after conducting the activity. This led to many conversations regarding the role and perception of libraries and librarians within the school district. The Talk portion is more about self-reflection and identifying what the individual user of the kit has done or could do to address any questions, concerns, or innovations inspired by the Think portion. The Target portion provides a chart that helps to develop a deliverable action plan.

Looking at the chart in the Target section might seem a little intimidating, at first. It is a good exercise in identifying the small steps that can be taken by the user as they continue to innovate. It includes space to state exactly what the user is going to do, the timeline to accomplish it, the other people needed to be involved, and a follow-up plan. When I was working with Ms. Buckley on this worksheet, the Target portion didn't consist of anything elaborate. Since our conversation and experience with this activity had a focus on the perception of the library within the culture of the school and district, the action plan was to talk with the faculty and administrators about how the benefits of the library support institutional goals. The timeline for implementing these conversations could start almost immediately, and the follow-up plan was to continuously speak up about the connection between library services and student success.

Although the "Institutional Focus Areas" activity focuses more on identifying goals, it does introduce the concept of considering your stakeholders when you are thinking about your organization as a whole. The second activity in the kit is called "Stakeholders as the Heart of the Institution." There are subject headings that resemble the same stakeholders Everyday Advocacy identifies. *The Impact Starter Kit* includes a checklist that offers the chance to be more specific about each general category of stakeholders for an academic library and offers space for any missing characteristics to be added.

Since *The Impact Starter Kit* is designed to be used for academic libraries, the students heading includes items like high school and prospective students. The parents heading compares with the Everyday Advocacy–identified stakeholders, but the items listed would be different for a public or school library setting. With a few adaptations, this activity could be a useful tool to target youth services within a public library or for an organization like Simple Positive Play.

Everyday Advocacy identifies children of all ages as stakeholders.[4] If I were to adapt *The Impact Starter Kit* to better reflect the different categories of students, instead of trying to encompass the various types of college students, I would identify different categories of students through age seventeen. For the organization of Simple Positive Play, I would focus on breaking down the age groups for ages through third grade.

A youth public library worker could separate the age groups according to the programs already in place. For instance, one of the items listed on the checklist could be ages three to five to reflect the ages of children who attend story time or ages six to nine to reflect early elementary school students. The Search Institute[5] has identified forty developmental assets that children can acquire to help build positive relationships within the community. The four different age groups for these developmental assets include ages three to five; kindergarten through third grade, or ages six to nine; ages eight to twelve; and teens, or ages twelve to eighteen. There is an overlap in ages across these four groups, but the categories provide a way to separate all children into groups that will share similar milestones and interests. Just like *The Impact Starter Kit* can provide some overlap between the at-risk, honors, and first-year students as categories under the students heading.

Although the organization of Simple Positive Play encourages all people to find value in playing in a positive environment, the ages it focuses upon range from birth through third grade. One of the frequent concerns that families have shared with me at Simple Positive Play has been their child's access to play with other students. During the COVID-19 pandemic, many services were closed or restricted to reduce the risk of spreading the virus. Because of this, play dates, story times, daycare facilities, and play spaces were unavailable to parents of young children, leaving the children with little to no interaction with kids their own age. Meeting developmental milestones is a common concern among parents that visit the space the organization Simple

Positive Play provides. The "children of all ages" breakdown for Simple Positive Play would be reduced to birth to third grade and separated by the six stages of play.

The six stages of play include Unoccupied Play (ages zero to three months), Solitary Play (ages zero to two years), Spectator/Onlooker Behavior (two years), Parallel Play (two-plus years), Associate Play (three to four years), and Cooperative play (four-plus years).[6] Students within each of these stages of play can benefit from different resources and environments. Acknowledging that different age groups require different support opens the opportunity to collaborate with other stakeholders that have more of an expertise or access to resources meant for a particular stage.

The parents heading in the "Stakeholders at the Heart of the Institution" activity would need some adjustments to better describe the primary stakeholders in the youth public library environment and for the organization of Simple Positive Play. Instead of listing items like "Parents of First-Year Students" and "Parents of First-Generation Students," the items would need to change to items like "Parents of Children Ages 0–2" and the other various age groups in addition to recognizing single-parent households, foster parents, immigrant families, and other caregivers like grandparents. Everyday Advocacy acknowledges the different kinds of caregivers and families with specific needs such as those with physical or mental disabilities, immigrant families, and those within the LGBT community.[7]

For the organization of Simple Positive Play, parents also serve as volunteers who contribute to the organization and operation of the space. The activity in *The Impact Starter Kit* has a heading titled "Library," which includes the various departments that influence and are associated with the operation of an academic library. The volunteers at Simple Positive Play would fall into this category in a restructured activity designed for spaces like Simple Positive Play. Identifying some parents as stakeholders, and as parents whose children use the space, provides an incredible amount of insight regarding the experience of others who use the space.

Everyday Advocacy identifies educational institutions and organizations serving youth as the remaining primary stakeholders besides students and parents. These stakeholders can include the variety of types of schools, home schools, teachers, and childcare providers but can also include organizations like Parents as Teachers or those that provide a professional who works one on one with students and parents in the child's home. Parent educators in the Parents as Teachers organization are able to monitor a child's development and identify whether the child is meeting developmental milestones. They also provide age-appropriate activities for parents to implement without the assistance of a teacher or an educator. The organization of Simple Positive

Play sometimes serves as a setting for monitoring behavior for an organization that works closely with families who suspect their child to be on the autism spectrum. Simple Positive Play has been able to provide a space for observation and the availability of a variety of resources has enabled the professional to develop specific circumstances to monitor such as using the games to view how the child takes turns or using puzzles to witness how a child navigates putting a puzzle together.

Children's performers like musicians, puppeteers, and storytellers can also be considered stakeholders. When I was a youth services librarian, the library system I worked for would frequently enlist the talents of performers and educational organizations to present engaging programs to children in the community. Some performers who would present at the library would travel from outside of the state to showcase different animals or perform. Some performers were specialists in presenting science concepts in ways that may be difficult for a youth library worker to achieve in consideration of their other job responsibilities. Valuing the contributions these performers bring to the library can also lead to collaborations and expose families to information and entertainment they might not otherwise have access to experience due to obstacles including, but not limited to, cost and travel.

The Impact Starter Kit includes many more categories in the "Stakeholders as the Heart of the Institution"[8] activity, including institutional offices; administrators; local, state, and national communities, and more. Some of these remaining categories in *The Impact Starter Kit* fall more under the concept of secondary stakeholders or those who benefit from the services provided, although not directly.

The directions in *The Impact Starter Kit* instruct users to check off all the relevant stakeholders to the institution and identify and rank the top five to create the core institutional stakeholder list. Using this activity as a guide to identify stakeholders helps users identify potential influencers and partners. The headings include populations that one might not immediately consider when referring to stakeholders and broaden the possibilities for collaboration with others who share similar focuses and goals. In fact, one of the responses to the Think portion of the T^3 process at the end of the activity resulted in Ms. Buckley becoming curious about just how many people could influence the library, wondering who is putting the most pressure on the success of libraries and even coming to the realization that local businesses could be stakeholders for the library, too.

The Impact Starter Kit includes several more activities related to stakeholders, but the final activity I am going to highlight is "Activity #6: Stakeholder Help Study,"[9] which is categorized within the theme of listening. This activity is not one that I completed as part of my project in graduate school with Ms. Buckley. However, it is an intriguing activity to review because of its simplicity. This activity guides users in conducting a simple interview that consists of a prompt followed by two questions. The prompt is, "Remember the last time the library or a librarian helped you. What did you get? What did that help enable you to do?"

As youth library workers, we are aware of what we do day-to-day, but it is sometimes difficult to assess whether library users are finding our efforts useful or helpful. Providing opportunities for feedback allows us to gather greater insight into their perception of the library and its resources. Much of the work for this activity lies within analyzing the responses of the stakeholders and recognizing the common responses gathered after each interview. This activity also encourages the user to consider helpful resources they would expect the stakeholder to mention but didn't. The activity then asks the user to think about other organizations that could also benefit from the results of this exercise. Of course, engaging in the T^3 process afterward leads to more opportunities to analyze what the user has learned and how this information can be used to enhance existing or implement new library services.

The Ferguson Municipal Library is located less than a mile away from where Simple Positive Play operates. There is also a large county library located within five miles of Simple Positive Play. The space and resources we are able to provide meet a different need for stakeholders than can be provided at any other local community entity. Our space is free and small but provides a safe environment for play and exploration that includes being loud at times. The placement of the building at January-Wabash Park provides a walking trail around a lake and access to a newly renovated, accessible playground within walking distance. Although the trajectory of Simple Positive Play still remains unknown, the target has never been to replace the amount of resources and services provided by other local organizations. The goal is to work collaboratively to reinforce positive resources in the community. The talents and efforts of the local libraries and the support of the community helps Simple Positive Play to stay in operation. Simple Positive Play wasn't created by one person; it was created by a collection of stakeholders offering their talents and support in ways that felt most comfortable to them.

NOTES

1. Everyday Advocacy, "Identify Key Stakeholders," American Library Association, April 10, 2013, https://www.ala.org/everyday-advocacy/engage/identify-key-stakeholders.

2. Megan Oakleaf, *Academic Library Value: The Impact Starter Kit* (Syracuse, NY: Dellas Graphics, 2012).

3. Oakleaf, *Impact Starter Kit*, 1.
4. Everyday Advocacy, "Identifying Key Stakeholders."
5. "The Developmental Assets Framework" Search Institute, accessed November 25,2022, https://www.search-institute.org/our-research/development-assets/developmental-assets-framework/.
6. "How Kids Learn to Play: 6 Stages of Play Development," Pathways, accessed November 25, 2022, https://pathways.org/kids-learn-play-6-stages-play-development/.
7. Everyday Advocacy, "Identifying Key Stakeholders."
8. Oakleaf, *Impact Starter Kit*, 2.
9. Oakleaf, *Impact Starter Kit*, 6.

10

Assessment and Impact

In this chapter, we're going to revisit the design-thinking process, more specifically, the defining, prototyping, and testing stages of design thinking. Rachel Ivey Clarke, Ann Rosenblad, and Satyen Amonkar reported in their article "Design Thinking and Methods in Library Practice and Graduate Library Education"[1] that librarians are most familiar with the empathizing and brainstorming stages but less engaged with the defining, prototyping, and testing stages. Design thinking is an iterative process rather than a linear one. In theory, moving from a stage of understanding the stakeholders or library users and advancing to the point where you can test and assess whether or not the project is useful or impactful is a journey along a path to a destination. In practice, the design-thinking process is more complicated and requires those implementing the design-thinking process to frequently revisit different stages before reaching the point where assessments can take place. Even though the design-thinking process isn't necessarily experienced in a sequential manner, each element needs to be included for the process to be used effectively.

Without the defining stage, there isn't a clear way of knowing whether or not the problem-solving strategies and program or service implemented are actually meeting any objectives or community needs. The defining stage is more than just identifying a problem, but it also includes defining your, or your organization's, objectives, and the mission statement is a great place to start.

The mission of Simple Positive Play is to facilitate playful learning experiences for young people and their families while also promoting an engaged and informed community. The initial objective when establishing this mission statement was to establish a positive environment or contribute to existing environment activities that promoted self-guided play. The organization started doing this by temporarily setting up playful experiences in community spaces like community food truck nights and festivals, an art studio, and, of course, my parents' driveway. When I, as the founder of Simple Positive Play, started collaborating with a parent in North St. Louis County, the objective changed. This parent's goal was to develop a local play space for her and her family to safely play indoors. The new objective became to establish a more permanent space to host play sessions for families.

Although this new goal supported the mission statement for Simple Positive Play, it wasn't SMART. This isn't a reflection of intelligence of any of the parties involved. SMART in this instance stands for Specific, Measurable, Achievable, Relevant, and Time-Bound.[2] To address the "S" for Specific, some aspects of the initial goal were somewhat specific and relevant but the goals were more focused on personal aspirations than organizational ones. Going into the endeavor, we weren't really sure whether or not the idea was achievable. However, it was a place to start. As we started to work on this goal, we discovered different obstacles to overcome. One of which was becoming an official 501(c)(3) nonprofit organization. At this time, I wasn't sure whether or not I wanted to establish a nonprofit organization or if I just wanted to use my free time to volunteer my services in a way that promoted self-guided exploration. Even planning to become an official 501(c)(3) nonprofit organization generated questions about which forms to complete and funding the application process. After doing some research, we were able to determine that we qualified to complete the 1023-EZ form. This form is significantly shorter than the 1023 long form used to establish nonprofits with a gross income of over $50,000. The application filing fee is less expensive, and the turnaround time from submitting the application and being granted nonprofit status was shorter as well.

Assessing whether we achieved the goal was very binary; either we created a space or we didn't. Determining whether we were holding true to our mission statement was, and is always, a question that remains at the forefront of decisions and goals we make for the future. Was our space designed for young people and their families in a way that provided a positive learning experience? Were we promoting an engaged and informed community? And how do we know that? More importantly, how do we share with others that we are achieving this goal?

It was difficult to determine what the space for families would look like considering we were not initially sure of what space we would be working within, what furniture we would have access to, and what funding would be available to us to develop the space. One of the first setups we generated in an indoor space was in the basement of a community space located in a park in Florissant, Missouri. The space was split between a lobby-like area outside of the restrooms and a small meeting space. The floors were laminated, and we were not allowed to post anything on the walls. Since the space was used for other engagements, like overflow for weddings taking place on the upper level or meetings, we had to be mindful of removing all or most of our supplies when we were allowed to use the space. Anticipating how exactly we'd use the space provided by the City of Ferguson allowed for more creativity since we would be given access to most of the building with the exception of the kitchen area that we would sometimes share with the pool.

When we gave our presentation to the Ferguson City council regarding use of the space at January-Wabash Park, we were encouraged to focus on an age range instead of stating that we were a space for young people of all ages. We determined that our focus would be on children from ages birth through nine years of age. This added specificity to our objective in a few different ways. Instead of focusing on providing space and playful resources for young people of all ages, our objective changed to developing the building at January-Wabash Park into a space with playful resources for young people ages birth to nine years of age and their families.

Now that we had a better definition of what our goal was, it became easier to determine what resources would be accessible within the space. The building that Simple Positive Play operates out of started as an empty space, once the leftover furniture from the building's previous use was removed. In trying to design the space, we were limited in the number of resources available for us to use. We had seating for adults in addition to tables and chairs in the kitchen area but that was it as far as furniture was concerned. For creative project supplies, I had acquired a collection of art supplies and books that I had used when I was setting up temporary play spaces in my parents' driveway and the art studio. We were able to purchase some toys using funds from a generation donation that included enough to replace the carpet and other toys were donated by local parents willing to part with their child's toys that were no longer being used.

We were able to better define our objectives in a way that invited more people to provide helpful assistance. People became aware of what we were trying to accomplish and offered more monetary donations and resources like a futon for adults, seating for children, books, and art supplies. By specifying our intentions, we were able to develop a board of directors and complete the necessary paperwork to become a nonprofit organization that provides playful resources and learning experiences for children and their families.

The "M" in SMART goals refers to the ability of the goal to be measurable. Our only unit of measurement was to hope that families would utilize the playful space we developed. Through the other, more temporary spaces where Simple Positive Play facilitated playful experiences, we knew that families were interested in having the resource. We determined this mainly from informal conversations with participants. We didn't have a specific number of participants that we were hoping to attract. This was, again, another binary approach to assessing our success; either people came to the space or they didn't.

The "A" in SMART stands for "Achievable." Once we were granted use of the building in Ferguson, Missouri, we had already accomplished one of our main objectives. When our objective changed to providing an indoor space with playful resources for children from birth through age nine, it seemed like a more focused and achievable goal.

As far as being "Relevant," which is the "R" in the SMART acronym, we were aware that there were not many places in the North St. Louis County area where parents could take their children for indoor play. The local libraries were available, but other indoor children's gyms and play spaces within stores and restaurants were no longer available. Additionally, other stand-alone play spaces required admission fees, which could be an obstacle for families with limited income. We also believed, and still do believe, that access to creative opportunities that encouraged and promoted safe, self-guided exploration for young people was and is a positive asset to the community.

The "T" in SMART stands for "Timely" or "Time-bound." I mentioned before that we didn't have a timeline for establishing an indoor space for children and their families. We were intent on moving forward with our plans as opportunities became available to us. The only circumstances when time was relevant to the way we assessed our open-play sessions was whether or not anyone showed up for play during our operational hours.

Defining and redefining one objective helped us to add structure to our endeavors, but it took time to make it specific, measurable, achievable, relevant, and timely. However, once we acquired the space, there was the issue of how to develop the space so that it was a positive environment for playful experiences. We brainstormed items that would promote imaginative play with trains, food, and costumes. We also knew that we would have a variety of art supplies for participants to use to make open-ended art projects. We did not know if we were placing items in the space that children and their families would enjoy. Every open-play session we hosted became an opportunity to prototype.

Prototyping in the traditional use of the design-thinking process involves developing an inexpensive version of the product to determine areas that need improvement or support. At the space developed for Simple Positive Play, we began by experimenting with resources we already had in addition to community donations. We spoke to children and families about other resources they would like to see in the space and started purchasing those items.

The space has gone through multiple iterations as new materials were added and as we observed the way that participants were using the supplies. We had to spend a lot of time figuring out how to organize the material so that it was accessible to participants and not hidden in boxes, cabinets or storage rooms. We just recently changed over the back storage area by putting up a curtain to maximize space. The hallway contains a countertop, and it used to be a hard place to incorporate. It has now been transformed into a book nook complete with child-sized furniture. This arrangement was influenced by participant input.

Libraries have used the design-thinking process to design spaces.[3] However, the process of prototyping can also be used to develop programming by implementing an aspect of the program on a smaller scale. While working at the library, I started to use volunteers and the Teen Advisory Group to design programs. The library system had a collection of round robots called Spheros in the youth services collection for staff to use in programs. The collection also contained a mini-golf kit and iPads to control the Spheros. I had an idea to create a mini golf with Spheros program for teens, but I wasn't sure if it would be possible. This youth services collection was housed at the headquarters library located about fifteen miles away from my branch and available for delivery to my branch through the library's delivery department. I coordinated the delivery of the supplies I thought I might need to use for the program during a time when I knew I'd also have a few volunteers available. I shared with the teens the idea for the program and asked them to test it out.

Even though I was vaguely familiar with the resources I'd be using for the program, observing the students play with the mini-golf kit with the Spheros helped me to recognize things I would need to prepare. For instance, not all of the obstacles designed to use with the mini-golf kit were suitable for use with the Spheros, so I was able to customize the kit to fit with the needs of the program. Prototyping the event gave me an opportunity to play with the application on the iPad that controlled the Spheros so that I would be better able to instruct and assist program participants. After the volunteers helped to prototype the event, I invited them to volunteer during the program since they were now familiar with the resources that were going to be used. Although those volunteers were not available during the scheduled event, providing the opportunity for those volunteers to obtain additional service hours by sharing their knowledge with others was something I was happy to offer.

Another example of using volunteers to prototype programs was in designing a program for National Learning Day. My plan was to challenge participants to create board games using found materials and scrap supplies that I placed in a gallon Ziploc bag. I had two volunteers prototype this activity during their volunteer shift one evening. Initially, the volunteers were instructed to create a game individually. After they had accomplished that task and shared their game with one another, I challenged them to create a game together. This provided insight as to whether the materials provided would be sufficient for building a game. Since the prototyping took place in the supply room, versus the programming room, I had plenty of access to additional supplies to consider using for the program. Using what I learned through the prototyped program, I was able to better prepare and present the board game challenge program on National Learning Day.

The organization of Simple Positive Play has presented a few special events that I wouldn't consider programs. We've celebrated the new year with a few "Noon Year's Eve" parties, and we've hosted a "Glow Party" too. Hosting a program where we can share information and engage in an activity in a more organized way is a little difficult to envision because the collection is distracting. Additionally, when Simple Positive Play is open, we don't expect people to show up at a specific time. There are so many parents who show up and say, "Sorry we're late!" But, as long as they are there during the operating hours, they are never late. They may be later than they wanted to arrive, but it certainly doesn't warrant an apology.

Much of the way that Simple Positive Play has grown has been through trial and error. However, incorporating an assessment plan would help to streamline the process of implementing and reflecting on programs in order to share and improve future offerings. In Megan Oakleaf's *Academic Library Value: The Impact Starter Kit*,[4] she provides an exercise to help academic libraries think critically about creating an assessment plan. Exercise #25[5] examines fears, challenges, and barriers involved in considering an assessment plan like the lack of time, funds, and support. Even if one were so overwhelmed by the challenges that may face the development of an evaluation method and select every challenge listed, the worksheet instructs the user to focus and analyze two of them. The questions that follow, after selecting the challenges to focus on, include taking inventory of strategies and previous education along with potential collaborations and partnerships that may assist with the assessment process. One section of the worksheet lists strategies as action words to motivate the worksheet user. Some of the strategies listed include educate, collaborate, and start small. This tool works to help the user start simply by recognizing, defining, and anticipating obstacles that might reveal themselves and potentially prevent the implementation of an assessment plan from moving forward.

This worksheet, although designed for academic librarians, can be a useful tool for youth public library workers to examine the way that we assess both individual and reoccurring programs and the structure of the department. Two of the challenges on the worksheet that really resonated with me are the lack of time and the lack of staff resources. It seems like I was always running from one program or project to another. If I wasn't trying to plan for a program, I was setting up, implementing, or presenting a program, planning an outreach event, organizing the collection, or cleaning up from previous events. It is rewarding to have a day full of work to do, but I didn't really recognize the importance of intentionally reflecting on things I had already completed. We kept track of the attendance at each program, and there were also program feedback forms to complete after programs presented by outside performers. There was even a point in time when we were encouraged to complete program assessment forms for our story time programs.

Statistics are a good way of keeping track of how many participants were present in the program, but it didn't tell the complete story of what was happening within the program. The performer reviews made sense because it was a way for the youth services department to determine whether a performer was worth hiring again. The story time evaluation had potential, but there was little accountability when it came to completing them. There was someone from the Youth Services Department who visited one of my story times who mainly said I did a good job, which is nice, but didn't provide any feedback that seemed useful in helping me to improve or alter the program. Additionally, there were forms for the branch managers to utilize but I never had a manager complete the form after viewing one of my story time programs.

In my experience, there was a bit of a disconnect between who was providing evaluations and what those evaluations were going to be used for. There wasn't a clear communication of why we were completing evaluations other than it seemed like a good idea with some potential. There wasn't any excitement about assessing programs to determine areas where youth library workers could use more support either through different resources or more education. Being excited about completing paperwork and being evaluated is a difficult thing to ask, but I do believe that if there was a more complete picture of what these evaluations would represent, they could have been viewed more as a useful tool than as busywork or, worse, as a way of negatively criticizing hard work. If it was presented as a concerted effort to identify ways to improve our story times, I might have been more eager to complete the forms. If no one was going to look at the forms anyway, I had a hard time justifying the time it took to complete them.

In the *Impact Starter Kit*, Activity #37[6] guides users of the kit through planning for assessment. These worksheets are not very long. This particular worksheet is simply a checklist of assessment plan components. It includes an overview section that encourages users to think about the purpose of the assessment plan and links to institutional focus areas. The links to strategic documents encourage users to think about the mission statement, strategic plan, and standards. One of the sections that was missing in my experience of assessments but included on this checklist is "Closing the Loop." Closing the loop includes figuring out what to do with the information gathered during the assessment and a reflection of how the assessment process itself might need to be adjusted to better provide the information being sought.

Considering outcomes and the way they will be measured and shared is also a part of this checklist. For each outcome selected, there is a list of other information to consider like target populations, responsibilities, and pilot recommendations, which can be used to prototype programs and the way that assessments are executed. The work and effort completed before the assessment plan starts can help guide decisions and promote the use of the assessment plan before it is ever implemented. It provides opportunities to alter and adjust the plan for individual organizations and is not a "one size fits all" approach to assessment. This worksheet illustrates that assessment is more than filling out a form, but it has the potential to influence the way we consider the time we spend reflecting on our own job performance and work to show how we make an impact.

The final activity I'll refer to out of the *Impact Starter Kit* is Activity #36: "Keeping Impact Simple."[7] The goal of this activity is to "articulate library impact clearly and succinctly." Unlike some of the other worksheets I have mentioned that include reflections using a checklist, this worksheet has five open-ended questions and space to complete written reflection answers. Two of the most thought-provoking questions are, "Does evidence of the impact exist?" and "Is this evidence shared with stakeholders?" On the surface, these two questions can be answered with a simple "yes" or "no." For the worksheet to be more useful, taking the time to reflect on these questions can help to generate a better approach to communicating how library services and programs provide an asset to the community. Providing evidence of your positive contributions will help develop a much more comprehensive story to share with current and potential stakeholders.

The concept of providing evidence to justify my work with developing the organization of Simple Positive Play to others isn't always in the forefront of my mind. Working with the community to create a space for free access to playful resources is, personally and professionally, very satisfying. I'm motivated by the stories I'm told by parents who visit the space and share how happy they are with the option of being able to bring their children to a safe place to engage with other children and play with toys and art supplies they may not have at home. Reflecting on questions regarding evidence has led me to reevaluating how we use our website and finding more opportunities for participants of all ages to record feedback and to actively participate in the testing and evaluation of the space's resources and services.

The Connected Learning Alliance has developed a playlist of videos titled, "Evaluating Connecting Learning Experiences" and provides information to consider when developing evaluation strategies and collecting data. Determining how and why you are collecting data helps to structure what questions you ask participants and how they respond. One of the videos in the playlist is titled "Designing Talkback Boards (Video 3),"[8] and it guides viewers on how to use talkback boards to collect feedback. Talkback boards consist of specific prompts that allow for participants to respond using a closed-ended "sticky dot" method or an open-ended "sticky note" method. In the closed-ended method, participants are provided with several prompts and asked to place a sticky dot or sticker within the spaces of the prompts they most identify with. The example featured in the video was designed to test if participants were interested in learning more about the information presented in the program or if they would prefer to do something different. Participants were provided with the main statement of "Next time I want to," and then provided four different options where they could place their sticker to indicate their answer. The possible answers included an option to do the exact same thing while other choices included enhancing what they've learned or trying something completely different. The video also stressed the importance of framing your options so that they were neutral and didn't skew overly positive or overly negative. This is reflected in the talkback board including the option of "This was a one-time situation" as an answer as it reflects not wanting to try this program again without expressing that the participant had a negative experience.

The open-ended approach to a talkback board includes displaying a prompt and asking participants to respond by recording their suggestion on a self-adhesive note and adding it to the display. The prompts for this type of talkback board also need to be specific and ask something that participants would be interested in influencing. A potential open-ended prompt for the organization of Simple Positive Play could be to ask for input regarding the collection of sensory toys. On the other hand, a closed-ended prompt could provide prompts to determine whether sensory toys are a priority for participants who visit the space. Both talkback boards could later lead to a survey with more specific types of sensory toys that Simple Positive Play would be willing to include in the collection.

The complete design-thinking process includes not just the ability to empathize and brainstorm but to critically think about the purpose and intent of the product or service you're creating and the ability to explore innovative ideas on a smaller scale before implementing, testing, and evaluating your efforts. The final chapter of *Design Thinking for Libraries: A Toolkit for Patron-centered Design* is titled "Getting to Scale"[9] and is all about how to grow the idea to where it can be replicated in similar environments. Simple Positive Play is currently working on developing a strategic plan that includes work on becoming more visible to the community and working harder to collaborate, engage with families, and share the story of Simple Positive Play. We've learned quite a lot from our attempts so far, and developing a more focused plan will give us the structure to expand the way we can connect people with information and playful resources. The defining, prototyping, and testing stages of design thinking represent the "play" in the concept of simple, positive play. It is similar to learning and adapting the rules of a game or activity and playing a practice round before the official game begins.

NOTES

1. Rachel Ivy Clarke, Ann Rosenblad, and Satyen Amonkar, "Design Thinking and Methods in Library Practice and Graduate Library Education," *School of Information Studies-Faculty Scholarship*, 2019, https://surface.syr.edu/istpub190.

2. "Develop SMART Objectives," Centers for Disease Control and Prevention, https://www.cdc.gov/publichealthgateway/phcommunities/resourcekit/evaluate/develop-smart-objectives.html.

3. Clarke, Rosenblad, and Amonkar, "Design Thinking and Methods in Library Practice and Graduate Library Education, 5.

4. Megan Oakleaf, *Academic Library Value: The Impact Starter Kit* (Syracuse, NY: Dellas Graphics, 2012).

5. Oakleaf, *Academic Library Value*, 25.

6. Oakleaf, *Academic Library Value*, 37.

7. Oakleaf, *Academic Library Value*, 36.

8. Connected Learning Alliance, "Designing Talkback Boards (Video 3)," YouTube Video, January 4, 2019, 10:02, https://youtu.be/tSDP7LbGHAY.

9. IDEO, *Design Thinking for Libraries: A Toolkit for Patron-centered Fesign*, 102–116.

11

A Simple Look at Programming

Library programming was a major component of my work as a youth public librarian. I was hired at a time when there were many structural changes happening within the library and I was able to learn and grow as the library changed policies and focused more on youth programming and services. Before I was hired, the duties of programming for youth were met by library assistants who had a multitude of different tasks to tend to on a daily basis. Upon my hiring, I was the first person whose sole responsibility was to focus on services for young people ages zero to eighteen and their families.

Although I had experience in hosting programs as a resident assistant in college and I had many experiences in theater that taught me how to think of production components, I had a lot to learn about implementing library programs.

WHAT IS PUBLIC LIBRARY PROGRAMMING?

In 2017, the Institute of Museum and Library Services awarded a grant to the American Library Association to develop a project called the National Institute for Library Public Programming Assessment (NILPPA).[1] The goals of this project are to analyze the data regarding library programs and then identify and define different characteristics shared by library programs in the United States. In one of NILPPA's news updates published on the website Programming Librarian, the group sought to define a public library program and concluded that a library program is an "intentional service or event in a social setting, developed proactively to meet the needs or interests of an anticipated target audience, at least some of whom attend by choice."[2]

This definition is used to apply to programs at various types of libraries including academic, K–12 school libraries, public libraries, and special libraries. I think it is natural to want to think about public library programming for young people to be similar to creating a lesson plan for a classroom, but the content presented in a library program has its own unique characteristics. The definition explains that library programs are social experiences, and while there is a fair amount of socializing that occurs in the classroom, the developers of the public library programming definition chose to list the description of "social setting" as one of the first characteristics. The use of the words "intentional" and "proactively" implies that there was time spent considering the relevance and purpose of a particular event or program. The last item mentioned in the definition is that people attend the library program by choice. For young people, they rarely have complete control over their own schedule; however, their parents and caregivers are responsible for making sure that students attend any out-of-school activities. The programs designed for young people have to appeal not only to the young people in attendance but also to the guardians that bring the young people to the program.

NILPPA researchers also developed a list of outcomes that represent the various library programs that take place across the United States. These outcomes include:

- Participants learn new knowledge.
- Participants learn new skills.
- Participants change their attitudes.
- Participants change their behaviors.
- Participants gain awareness of library resources, services, or programs.
- Participants have fun or are inspired.
- Together, libraries and participants build stronger and healthier communities.[3]

Additionally, NILPPA identified nine core library programming competencies. The competencies include having organizational skills, knowledge of the community, interpersonal skills, event planning skills, creativity, content knowledge, and financial skills. Additionally, public library workers who implement programs need the ability to conduct outreach, implement marketing strategies, and accurately evaluate programs. [4]

PROGRAMMING FOR AGES ZERO TO SEVENTEEN

I was hired to work at the library about one month before the beginning of the annual Summer Reading Club program. If you are not familiar, the Summer

Reading Club program is one of the busiest times of year for a youth public librarian. At that time, the library system invested in hiring professional presenters for weekly performances, and the branch scheduled many programs to take full advantage of the opportunity to draw families into the library since school was not in session. It is also a time when the library implemented reading incentive programs that included distributing prizes at different milestones. I had not experienced anything quite like it growing up, so it was an entirely new experience for me.

After the busy programming and library traffic of the summer, I was expecting a portion of that attendance to continue throughout the school year. However, it appeared as though the community wasn't necessarily looking to the library for programs during the school year. In fact, I would have conversations with community members who were unaware that library programs continued all year long. One of the things I began to look at was the availability and consistency of programs for ages zero to seventeen.

SCHEDULING PROGRAMS

When I first arrived, there was a weekly story time program and a monthly Teen Advisory Group (TAG) meeting that were scheduled on a regular, consistent basis. Other programs for school-aged children and programs featuring special guests or performers were presented when the availability of time and space coincided with the schedule of the library. Frequently, in my situation, the special guests and presenters were coordinated through the youth library staff at the main library branch, and they would work with all twenty branches of the library system to schedule an activity. Although I had some control over when these programs were to be presented and was able to select several possible dates for these programs to occur, I didn't always get my first choice. Scheduling programs in this manner was an incredible convenience because, in addition to assisting with acquiring the performers, the main library branch would also arrange for the publicity associated with the events.

My library system was very supportive of the individual branches scheduling their own programs, too. There were many times when I would come up with an idea like a craft project or science experiment that I had learned was successful at other branches and tried to implement them at my own location. I would put in publicity requests for the communications department, advertise in the monthly branch brochure, and share the upcoming program with the participants that came to other programs. However, there were many times when all the effort to promote the program yielded little to no attendance.

I began to think about programs in terms of consistency. Instead of focusing on what I would consider "one off" programs or a single program without any relationship to another program, I tried to consider themes or regularly scheduled programs that would make it easier to incorporate into a busy schedule. For instance, story time happened at the same time every week. Thursdays were story time days, and it was easy to promote at outreach events and in conversations with library users.

Having a pattern for programming days also assisted with reserving the programming space for programs. Our library system had a window of time that was reserved for library staff to reserve meeting rooms for programming before opening the scheduling of meeting rooms to the rest of the public. Obtaining the room at the desired times before the rooms were available for others to schedule significantly reduced scheduling conflicts and allowed me to have a better understanding of my own schedule.

FORMAT

In addition to patterns for scheduling programs, developing a pattern for the way I formatted each program made it easier to plan and organize my time. Story time was the first program that I implemented on a weekly basis, so I developed a format for this program first. All the other programs I've presented have been loosely based off the format I've used for story time.

Every program begins with introducing the program and sharing the agenda. For story time, my introduction is, "Welcome to story time! This program is intended for ages three to five, but, of course, anyone looking for a good story is welcome to join us. Today we are going to read stories, sing a few songs, and dance! After that, we'll move over to the tables for a fun activity. We'll have time to talk with our friends after the stories, but for now, I ask that we enjoy these stories together. If there is a time when you need to make some noise or take a break, feel free to go to the back of the room, into the hall, or enjoy the children's area and then come back in and join us when you're ready. Let's get started!"

I then transition into a movement song. One of my favorites to use for story time is the classic song "Head, Shoulders, Knees, and Toes." When I introduce the song, I'll say something like "Before we read stories, we have to make sure that you are all here. Your head, shoulders, knees, and toes!" Then we sing the song, pointing to the body parts as we go. I do the song multiple times. First at a regular pace, then at an extremely slow pace, and we finish up with going as fast as we can. Changing the tempo provides an opportunity to incorporate some information about the benefit of songs and how songs slow down language, enabling children to more clearly hear the different sounds in words. I then pair the song with The Learning Groove's version of "Head,

Shoulders, Knees, and Toes,"[5] which adds a little funk to the song. Before I play the song, I let participants know that the lyrics are slightly different from the traditional song and include directions to step and jump forward and backward. It also includes a direction to "Talk to the Hand." Not many children are familiar with this, so I demonstrate the move, which includes standing sideways with an outstretched arm with an open palm facing away from you and your other hand on your hip. After playing the song, we're ready for stories.

In addition to sharing expectations and welcoming participants, an introduction and song provides a buffer period for families to arrive. Getting a child out of the house with all their accessories to arrive at a location on time can be fraught with obstacles. Knowing that I want to maintain the room's attention when sharing a story and that families may not arrive right at the start time, the introduction allows me to engage with attendees while also providing grace for those who may have encountered unexpected situations on the way to the library. Even if those who come in later miss the announcement regarding expectations, if an incident does arise where a child or caregiver is being disruptive, I feel more confident and comfortable reminding the participants of the expectations and solutions. As a host, I want every guest to feel welcome in the space.

Transitioning from one story to another is something to consider. It is sometimes difficult, even for adults, to sit still for long periods of time. These transition times provide an opportunity to use movement songs, fingerplays, and props. Incorporating scarves, shakers, and flannel boards can be uncomfortable at first, but, after practice and time, they become easier to add to a story program. I'm a fan of using scarves. Even passing out scarves can be a task. I've witnessed scarves being handed out randomly. Another way to handle it is to invite students to the scarves bag to select their own. One story time presenter had the children close their eyes and put their heads down while the presenter dropped various scarves around them. When the children opened their eyes, they chose the scarf closest to them. My favorite song to start scarf play is "We Wave Our Scarves Together," which I learned from Jbrary.[6] It includes basic movements and gets us in the mood to work with the scarves. I may do another scarf song, or two, that may or may not fit the theme of the story time. It's viewed as a break. When it is time to put the scarves away, I have learned a rhyme that goes, "Shake your scarves high, shake your scarves low, shake your scarves fast, shake your scarves slow. Dance it on your shoulders, dance it on your head, dance it on your knees, then tuck it into bed. Goodnight scarf!"

After the stories and songs are complete, the program moves to a hands-on craft or activity. To prepare for this portion of the program, the tables are covered with tablecloths and the supplies are placed in the center of the table. I prefer placing all the components of the craft or activity in the center of the table, versus one item for each place setting at the table, because it was easier to set up. The collective pile of necessary supplies in one area on the table also made it quicker to clean up and provided opportunities for participants to share instead of having to worry about a box of crayons, glue sticks, and scissors for each participant.

Story times for children zero to two years old were called "Lap Time" in the library system where I worked. The format for these programs was similar to that of story time in that I welcomed and introduced the program to participants and sang a "Hello" song before we transitioned into stories, fingerplays, and songs. Evaluating books for this program is different than choosing books for story time. The younger children aren't likely to listen to a long story. I would approach the selection of books to use by finding books with few words, rhyming words, repeated phrases, and stimulating pictures. Incorporating flannel boards and fingerplays helped to engage the youngest of children. Having stories with repeated words or phrases allowed me to invite the parents to repeat after me. Lap time was also a great opportunity to incorporate scarves and tools like shaker eggs.

At the end of lap time, I would set out an assortment of toys and activities. I would also include a Play-Doh and coloring table. Some of these items would be placed in the corner of the room before stories began. In my introduction to this program, I acknowledged that it is very common for children this age to make noise and to get up and walk around. I reassured them that I was fine with standing up but wanted to make sure that everyone heard the stories. I invited them to play with the toys in the back of the room if they needed a distraction. I also made them aware that they could move to the hallway or children's area to relax, if need be, and join us back in the room whenever they were ready to return.

The main, planned portion of the program was over within fifteen to twenty minutes. However, acknowledging that it takes a lot of work to get a small child bundled and to the library, the play time for the kids lasted thirty-five to forty minutes. During play time, not only did the children get an opportunity to play around other children but also parents got the opportunity to meet their community and make connections with others.

Even though the content of a program for older kids is different, the structure of how I format the program is fairly similar. I start with an introduction where I welcome participants, talk about upcoming programs or new services, and outline the expectations of the program. The beginning of the program has a short presentation offering background information or inspiration to help generate ideas or support the hands-on activity. Sometimes I incorporate a variety of activities to increase the likelihood that participants engage in something they enjoy. At the end of the program, I try to leave time for students to share their creation before heading home.

Over time, I helped to increase the number of programs offered for elementary school students. In addition to the professional performers organized by the central youth services department, I started offering a monthly Kid's Book Club, a science-based program called Discovery Club, and an art-based program called Creative Space for Kids. The branch computer lab trainer also started hosting a Minecraft Club for kids in the branch's computer lab.

Minecraft Club and Creative Space for Kids were very open-ended in that there was little presentation before students were able to start engaging with the game or material. In Minecraft Club, it was important to communicate the expectations for playing with other participants. We learned from other youth specialists and lab trainers hosting the program and through our own experience that setting clear boundaries and consequences for not playing respectfully helped to ensure a smoother program. Creative Space for Kids was a program in which I would arrange an assortment of craft material on a table that I would refer to as a "craft buffet." Students were able to use the supplies available to create whatever they wanted to create. This program focused on open-ended art experiences for school-aged kids.

Inspired by an influx of technology available to youth services staff from the youth services collection, I began a program called Tech Tuesday. Our library collection consisted of access to things like Macbooks, video and audio equipment, and products like Makey Makeys, which is a fun tool that allows electrically conductive materials like bananas or Play-Doh to turn into buttons to control games or play music. We also had access to iPads, Ozobots, Spheros, a robot called Cozmo, and more. The equipment was shared with the other nineteen branches within the library system, and we were allowed to borrow them for a short period of time for programming purposes. At one point, much of the material was offered as kits in which the items were sorted by audio/visual material or robotics material. In my experience, it was difficult to offer all the items in the kits at one time. Many participants in my program didn't have regular access to these types of materials, so it took time to teach them how everything operated. Establishing Tech Tuesday allowed me to focus on one item in the collection at a time to not only introduce to the participants how the item worked but also to give students more of an opportunity to create with that particular piece of equipment.

Even when professional performers presented programs at the branch, I still viewed myself as the host. I would make sure that the room was prepared and welcome the performer to the space. Preparing the room included making sure the tables and chairs were set up correctly, the necessary technology was available, and a display with relevant library content was set up. I would also remain available to help greet visitors to the program and provide an introduction.

There were several times in which I would talk to high school students who thought that the Teen Advisory Group was an opportunity for me to offer guidance and advice to them versus an opportunity for them to advise us on different types of programs and resources they would be interested in participating in. It was with the help of teen volunteers that I was able to start formatting the Teen Advisory Group program in a way that was easy to duplicate from month to month. One teen volunteer was interested in presenting to the group himself. I would start off with an introduction and then he would ask some "Would You Rather...?" questions and share interesting facts like "This Day in History" to generate discussions. I'd get participant input on what kinds of programs they'd like to see at the branch, and we would work together to design what activities we could have at their program. Sometimes I would initiate a theme like "A Very Merry UN-Birthday," inspired by the story of *Alice's Adventures in Wonderland*,[7] or students would offer suggestions for various video game tournaments. Basic art supplies like colored pencils and paper were always available at each meeting and, although many kept doodling with their head down during the presentation portion, they still added input to the planning process. After the initial presentation, I also made games available or offered a special craft activity.

Teens in the area oftentimes needed to complete volunteer hours for school. When I first began, the branch offered a yearly book sale. I would frequently enlist the help of teen volunteers to help organize books for the sale. Eventually, the library changed the way they handled donations and discarded books and organizing books, for the book sale was no longer a volunteering option. I began offering volunteer hours for assisting within programs like Tech Tuesdays because it was nice to have more people available to help program participants learn how to use the technology and it seemed to be a task teen volunteers were willing to perform.

THEMES AND PROGRAM IDEAS

Themes for programs make it easier for me to focus on complementary content. I look for inspiration for program ideas from items in the collection and popular media. However, there are ways that a theme can be creatively restrictive. One mistake to avoid is selecting a theme before adequately checking to make sure there is enough content to fill a program. A theme should be a tool that helps define a program instead of adding more challenges. It should also be something that you'll enjoy presenting to others. If you find the theme interesting, it will be easier to portray that enthusiasm in the program.

Another way to discover potential themes for programming is through engaging in conversations with participants at programs and outreach events. Asking for feedback or input about previous programs can provide insight that may generate a program idea, too. Young people have large imaginations and may suggest an activity that seems too large for the library to implement. For instance, if a student suggested having the circus visit the library, it may be out of the budget to hire circus performers. There might not be a circus nearby or maybe the library doesn't have the space to host a traditional circus. However, that idea could inspire a circus-themed program in which participants design their own games or pretend to walk a balance beam that is a piece of duct tape in a line on the floor.

Other resources for themes and program ideas include looking at programs at different libraries and library systems. There have been many times when observing another librarian implement a program has inspired a new approach that I started to implement in my own programs. The Programming Librarian website is a catalog of various program ideas for all types of libraries. The blog even has an "Event Planning Checklist"[8] that can be used to help organize components of an event, especially for larger projects involving multiple people. Even if you are the only one using the checklist, it can encourage you to complete various tasks that will help you to be ultimately prepared for the program.

TIME

It can be easy to get carried away with the numerous possibilities for a library program. In an effort to create something memorable, you can develop something that is too complicated for the resources currently available to you. One major resource to consider is the amount of time you have available to you to plan, organize, and implement your program.

In an effort to be more organized with my time, I tried to budget how long it would take me to plan a regularly scheduled program like story time. I budgeted one hour of time to plan the program. This included choosing a theme or topic and deciding on the various resources that could be used to support the program. Preparing for the program was one hour, too, and included ordering or shopping for supplies, taking care of any preparation for the craft that might make it easier for participants to engage with the project, and gathering the resources needed to implement the program and create a display.

I also budgeted one hour each for setting up the program, implementing the program, and breaking down the program. In my branch, we had a programming room that had some storage space for supplies. We also had a larger space where the bulk of our programming supplies were located. Gathering the supplies and transporting them to the programming space didn't take a lot of time, but it still was a part of setting up and also breaking down and cleaning up the program afterward.

I didn't always need a full five hours to plan a particular program because I could alter a program I had implemented before or use the resources shared by another program. Sometimes planning a program was simply easier to plan. Budgeting my time helped me to find a way of organizing the way I organized my day. However, this format may look different under different circumstances.

SPACE

Something to consider when planning programs is the programming space. Can you move tables and chairs to best fit the needs of your program? In the programs that were for younger ages, we found that the tables for the programming room were too tall for young people. The library branch bought smaller tables to use within those programs so that younger people had an easier and safer time coloring, playing with Play-Doh, or engaging in another activity like completing a puzzle.

Another example of examining the space and arranging it the way that best suits the program involves the meeting space that I used to use for story time before the branch was renovated. The room was set up so that all the chairs faced the same wall with the entry door. I found that when I hosted programs, participants would become distracted by everyone who came into the room after the program began. Facing the chairs to the opposite wall wasn't an option because the opposite wall was made of all windows that looked at the parking lot and a swimming pool, which would also be a distraction. Another obstacle for the space was a series of support pillars that could potentially block a participant's line of sight. After some careful planning, branch staff and I were able to reconfigure the chairs for story time so that the chair and table arrangement limited distractions for the program.

One way to assess your space is to enter the room like one of your participants. When you walk in, try to take note of what you see first and what you feel when you enter the room. Have you created a welcoming environment? What could you do to make it more welcoming?

SNACKS

There are several things to consider when making the decision of whether to incorporate snacks into a program. Incorporating a snack might be a way to support a community need while also hosting an experience during a program. Sometimes we have snacks available at the organization of Simple Positive Play. However, with a limited budget, the decision becomes whether we want to spend our funds on more art materials and cleaning supplies or purchase more snacks. When there was an expectation of snacks available at open-play sessions, kids would frequently open multiple bags of snacks and much of it would go to waste. Offering food also adds items to preparation for the program and considerations for food allergies and sensitivity. For me, it worked best to offer snacks for special events. It is best to analyze your resources and community needs to determine what is best for your location.

Programming doesn't have to start off as complicated. Think of it as simply inviting the community into a hospitable space with useful and engaging information. More elements to your programs can be added as you become more comfortable. For instance, you could have children's music playing in the space before a program starts and as you are welcoming guests. You could incorporate a slideshow featuring flyers of upcoming events happening at your library or within your library system. In programs for younger children, you can start to incorporate things like scarves, shakers, flannel board stories, or parachute play. My experience has been to grow with my community by inviting them to participate in simple, positive play at the library.

NOTES

1. "About," National Impact of Library Public Programming Assessment, accessed November 25, 2022, https://nilppa.org/about/.

2. ALA Public Programs Office, "News: NILPPA Update: What is a Public Program, Anyway?" Programming Librarian, May 8, 2018, https://programminglibrarian.org/articles/nilppa-update-what-public-program-anyway.

3. B. Sheppard et al., *National Impact of Library Public Programs Assessment: Phase 1, A White Paper on the Dimensions of Library Programs & the Skills and Training for Library Program Professionals*, NewKnowledge Publication #IML.074.207.07 (Chicago: American Library Association & New Knowledge Organization Ltd., 2019), 8.

4. Sheppard et al., *National Impact of Library Public Programming Assessment*, 12.

5. "Head, Shoulders, Knees and Toes," The Learning Groove, accessed November 25, 2022, https://www.thelearninggroove.com/head-shoulders-knees—toes.

6. Jbrary, "We Wave Our Scarves Together: Storytime Song," YouTube Video, 1:49, https://www.youtube.com/watch?v=HvnQP2z7Z9M.

7. Lewis Carroll, *Alice's Adventures in Wonderland* (New York: Harper Designs, 2010).

8. Jessica C. Haas, "Blog: Event Planning Checklist," *Programming Librarian*, August 9, 2017, https://programminglibrarian.org/blog/event-planning-checklist.

12

The Continuing Evolution of Simple Positive Play

Simple, positive play is a concept that emphasizes acting on an idea in manageable steps, remaining optimistic about the eventual outcome, and not being afraid to learn from previous experiences. It also includes working with others to identify different areas of strength provided by various resources that are readily available and accessible.

The organization of Simple Positive Play began because I started to ask, "What if?" questions and experimenting with the different components of youth services in public libraries. Library service for young people wouldn't exist at all if it wasn't for those who dedicate their time and voices to showing that access to information for young people of all backgrounds is a right that should be withheld and supported. I used what I have previously experienced and learned about the needs and interests of the community and the dynamics of creating positive experiences for young people to develop an organization that focuses on promoting the same type of connectedness I feel the library represents.

The library represents connectedness in numerous ways. The resources that are available within a public library are there for the community to share with one another. The content of the resources share information, perspectives, stories, and artistic prowess. The programs connect community members to each other, and the librarians and public library workers are the facilitators of it all. Whether it is a librarian helping to connect a community member to the material by giving directions to the material's location or sharing a booktalk or recommendation, or the custodian who cleans, sets up meeting rooms for programs, and makes sure the building space is welcoming and inviting, public library workers create a space for connected learning.

When Simple Positive Play started, the main priority was to make creative material accessible to the community. In my parents' driveway in Louisiana, Missouri, I was trying to provide an activity that I would present at the library where I worked and the library in town wasn't currently offering in the same way. When I set up for more mobile events, I mainly focused on what I could fit in my car to be temporarily available for others to use and explore. Moving to the building in Ferguson, Missouri, I was able to consider other ways of making art supplies and creative resources available in a more permanent arrangement.

When I no longer had to focus my energy primarily on just getting the material to a location, I could toy around with how the material was configured to best accommodate the people who entered the space. The building that houses Simple Positive Play is a great space but, as with just about any building, it has limitations on what materials can be placed where. In the beginning, we were mainly hindered by what material we had available to us. We were able to borrow some furniture from the city of Ferguson, but it turned out that the furniture wasn't always being used appropriately. The lightweight, round stools were being used to roll on top of across the floor and presented as a safety risk. We initially filled up space with collapsible tunnels, alphabet puzzle mats made of interlocking foam and cardboard boxes. We also had a space dedicated to art supplies like paint, construction paper, fuse beads, markers, and more. We named this space the Mini Maker Lab.

As more people visited the space, I would frequently ask participants about what material they would like to see in the space. Participants began to not only make suggestions but also to bring donations. Several families offered to contribute books, crafty individuals donated art supplies, and one family donated a changing table for the restroom. Families brought in cars, trains, puzzles, and games to share with anyone who visited the space. Another family donated a play kitchen set they no longer had a use for. As I observed participants playing with certain toys and materials, I would use the monetary donations to purchase an upgrade to the play kitchen, activity tables, and foam climbers to help satisfy the community's expressed desire to have an indoor space to let kids climb and play.

After filling the main play space with play resources, the organization started focusing on making sure that there were play resources for the various age groups of children. We began getting more musical instruments, baby dolls, capes, and toys that promoted visual stimulation for the youngest of participants. The Mini Maker Lab started to include products that promoted circuitry like littleBits and Snap Circuits in addition to copper tape and LED lights.

The main play space in the building gets the most use. Observing play in this room, I can easily see how a configuration might not be the best and could require some adjustments. One of my favorite things to do is to sort and organize the toys, and participants in the space always challenge the organization. Instead of competing to keep things the way I originally situate material, I try to follow the lead of the participants and volunteers. Most people who visit the space want to help clean up before they leave, so organizing the space that makes it more apparent as to where things go not only contributes to keeping things organized but also enables others to feel invited to help put items away.

The Mini Maker Lab has been a different experience when it comes to organizing material so that it can be used. Although the various materials are organized in a way that is easily accessible, a frequent comment I've received from those who enter the space is that they don't know where to start. Some have suggested that I focus on one craft activity each time that we're open, but I've long felt that it takes away from the idea that all of the materials in the room are for participants to use. Additionally, activities that I would consider offering in the Mini Maker Lab might not be as comfortable for volunteers to host when they are operating the space.

The feedback I received regarding the Mini Maker Lab has been helpful in that it helped me to contemplate why a room full of art supplies wouldn't inspire endless amounts of creativity and imaginative innovation. I've established relationships with some of the participants who have expressed that they didn't know they could use everything that is available in the space. On the other hand, I've had participants use the material in ways that seemed wasteful, like emptying an entire bottle of glitter glue onto a single sheet of construction paper or filling a paper plate with paint only to paint three thin-lined circles.

The goal is to create an open-ended experience while also being considerate of the supplies. It is rare that a first-time visitor comes to the space and knows exactly what they would like to create or explore in the Mini Maker Lab. I'll frequently give a brief tour of the space and share how to use a particular item or game if the participants are not familiar. In this way, I'm able to introduce the supplies and welcome participants to use them, but there are more things that I can do to help others use the material available.

One project I began working on was a Simple Positive Play Pack. The intention for the play packs is to help families work together creatively at home. I created different bags that included a variety of art supplies like scissors, glue, and crayons. I also made simple suggestions on what to do with the materials supplied. I wanted this kit to be something that parents and caregivers could borrow and return. The main reasoning for returning the materials was to see if they were being used or if I was just giving out material. Handing out free supplies to the community isn't a negative thing, but it isn't a sustainable service that I can offer at this time.

Another iteration of the Simple Positive Play Packs emerged when I realized that I was taking a lot of time to develop the different kits. One kit would have a focus on cutting, with paper strips and scissors, while another one would focus on sewing with chenille stems, a plastic needle, beads, and a piece of plastic mesh. The kit that I created for collaging, however, was relatively easy to create and allowed for variability in the supplies. Each kit contained pompoms, stickers, buttons, glue sticks, and scissors, along with foam stickers or any other art supply or found object that could be used to collage. This idea transitioned into a collage kit that included a small, colored box of material full of items of the same color. For instance, the small, red box would include red pompoms, red chenille stems, red buttons, red foam squares, red felt, and red tissue paper. It also included red Play-Doh, scissors, and crayons.

Now it was time to test the new product and get some feedback. When I made the first play packs, I would offer them to families and encourage them to use the material and let me know what they thought about it. No one that I had given the packs to provided any feedback about the kits. Some people declined to take a kit because they didn't want to make a mess at home. I eventually put all the materials for the kits into cardboard boxes and promoted that they could use the material and store or return anything they didn't use. This wasn't an option when I was putting the kits in plastic bags. I received positive feedback for the collage kits, and I worked with one of the parents who tested one to add another component.

The benefit of collage kits was not only that it was easy to fill a box with craft items of the same color but also that it was easy for any volunteers to do the same. A new iteration of the project was developed to where parents and young people could not only take things home to create collages but also add contents to the box that shared the same color. One family took home a box of blue material and brought it back with pieces of fabric and blue craft supplies for the next person to use.

Many have suggested that I sell the kits. I was hesitant to start selling anything because I don't want anyone feeling pressured to buy anything when they visit Simple Positive Play in Ferguson, Missouri. However, developing the kits to raise awareness and funds to keep the space full of material is an option to take to community festivals or farmer's markets. To expand on the collaging and color coordinated theme of the kits, I organized all the material in the Mini Maker Lab by color, including LEGOs.

The concept of simple, positive play is a way to examine and implement programs and services that help to improve the community. It is a persistent way of thinking that motivates the way I approach being a youth services librarian. There are going to be projects and programs that don't play out according to the initial plan. It's important to recognize the parts of the plan that worked. Reflect on what could have been more successful and, most importantly, try again.

Simple Positive Play, the concept and the organization, was inspired by libraries and those who work tirelessly to promote curiosity and innovation. As a free resource located in large and small communities all over the country, libraries provide opportunities for joyful exploration. The library is a playground where young people can utilize what they know to explore their interests and youth public library workers help facilitate that exploration by developing welcoming spaces and hosting programs to showcase ideas.

Appendix

Photo Album of an Evolving Space

In 2015, I met with a parent in north St. Louis County who was interested in developing an indoor play space for children. She was aware of my experience at the library and with the periodic play sessions I hosted in my hometown. Through some of her connections, she became aware of an underutilized space in Ferguson, Missouri. It had previously served as the office for the Parks and Recreation Department. There was some damage to the building during the civil unrest in 2014 but it was minimal, with a broken window and a burn mark in the window frame. At the time that I toured the space, the Parks and Recreation offices had moved to a new building and there were remnants of cubicle walls stored in the space.

Upon getting permission from the city council to use the building, the Parks and Recreation Department agreed to paint the walls, replace the window, and deep-clean the floors. However, the space had served as an office with a considerable amount of foot traffic over the years, and some of that history remained evident in the marks that remained on the carpet.

An interested party visited the space to lend advice and offer encouragement. They also looked at the carpet and determined that it wasn't in ideal condition for young children to crawl around on. They requested that I obtain a quote to replace the carpet in the space. When I delivered the quote, they returned with a large donation that not only helped replace the carpet but also went toward purchasing the foam climbing equipment. Over time, as we gathered more donations, we were able to supply playful resources for visitors to the space.

Figure a.1. Simple Positive Play Building before new carpet. *Source*: Jennifer Ilardi

Figure a.2. Simple Positive Play Building after new carpet. *Source*: Jennifer Ilardi

Figure a.3. Simple Positive Play as of June 2022. *Source:* Geneva Crowe

The building is directly next to the local swimming pool. The kitchen of the building has access to the swimming pool area, and it was previously used for the birthday cake and presents portion of birthday parties hosted at the pool. Because Simple Positive Play essentially shares the space with the Parks and Recreation Department, it was our responsibility to clear out any of our art supplies anytime a birthday party was scheduled. Over time, birthday parties were no longer offered in the kitchen area, and Simple Positive Play was able to develop a more permanent collection in the space.

Much of the furniture in the space is easy to move, so areas of the space get reconfigured to either account for a better play space or for an additional resource to add to the collection. To this day, Simple Positive Play still shares the space with the Parks and Recreation Department. There are times when the space is used by volunteers during the summer's end regional swim meet or when city employees need a place to get cool during the July Fourth celebration. There is a mutual respect for the space and an understanding that we're all working together for a better community.

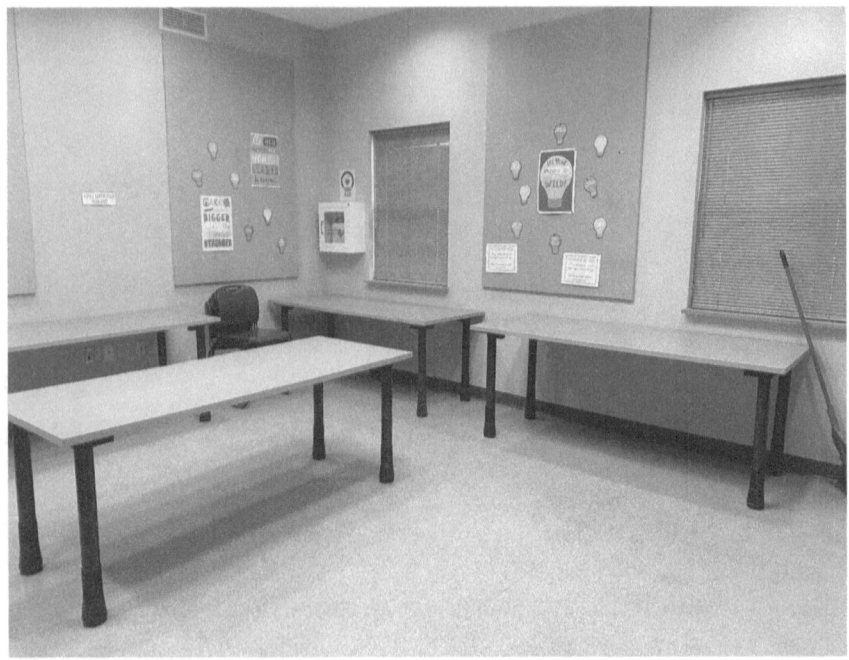

Figure a.4 Mini Maker Lab Empty *Source*: Jennifer Ilardi

Figure a.5 Mini Maker Lab June 2022 *Source*: Geneva Crowe

Figure a.6 Mini Maker Lab June 2022 *Source*: Geneva Crowe

Bibliography

ALA Public Programs Office. "News: NILPPA Update: What is a Public Program, Anyway?" Programming Librarian, May 8, 2018. https://programminglibrarian.org/articles/nilppa-update-what-public-program-anyway.
American Library Association. "Core Values of Librarianship." July 26, 2006. https://www.ala.org/advocacy/intfreedom/corevalues.
Association for Library Services to Children. "Competencies for Librarians Serving Children in Libraries." American Library Association, November 30, 1999. https://www.ala.org/alsc/edcareeers/alsccorecomps.
Barnett, Mac. *Extra Yarn.* New York: Balzar + Bray, 2012.
Bernier, Anthony. "Isn't It Time for Youth Services Instruction to Grow Up? From Superstition to Scholarship." *Journal of Education for Library and Information Science* 60, no. 2 (April 2019): 118–38. https://doi.org/10.3138/jelis.2018-0055.
Boggiano, Ann K., and Diane N. Ruble. "Competence and the Overjustification Effect: A Developmental Study." *Journal of Personality and Social Psychology* 37, no. 9 (1979): 1462–68.
Brosgol, Vera. *Leave Me Alone!* New York: Roaring Book Press, 2016.
Butler, Melissa. "Play as Truth." Fred Rogers Institute. Accessed September 25, 2022. https://www.fredrogersinstitute.org/resources/play-as-truth.
Carroll, Lewis. *Alice's Adventures in Wonderland.* New York: Harper Designs, 2010.
Casey, Teresa. "IPA Play in Crisis: Support for Parents and Carers." International Play Association, 2002. https://cdn.icmec.org/wp-content/uploads/2020/04/IPA-Play-in-Crisis-Booklet-for-parents-and-carers-2020.pdf.
Centers for Disease Control and Prevention. "Develop SMART Objectives." Accessed November 25, 2022. https://www.cdc.gov/publichealthgateway/phcommunities/resourcekit/evaluate/develop-smart-objectives.html.
Chicago Public Library. "YOUmedia." Accessed July 19, 2022. https://www.chipublib.org/programs-and-partnerships/youmedia/.

Clarke, Rachel Ivey, Ann Rosenblad, and Satyen Amonkar. "Design Thinking and Methods in Library Practice and Graduate Library Education." School of Information Studies-Faculty Scholarship 190 (2019). https://surface.syr.edu/istpub/190.

Clay, Rebecca A. "The Serious Business of Play." American Psychological Association, May 11, 2022. http://apa.org/topics/covid-19/children-unstructured-play.

Connected Learning Alliance. "Designing Talkback Boards (Video 3)." YouTube, January 4, 2019, 10:02. https://youtu.be/tSDP7LbGHAY.

Dam, Rikke Friis. "The 5 Stages in the Design-thinking Process." Interaction Design Foundation. Accessed June 2022. https://www.interaction-design.org/literature/article/5-stages-in-the-design-thinking-process.

David J. Spencer CDC Museum: In Association with the Smithsonian Institution. "CDC Museum COVID-19 Timeline." Centers for Disease Control and Prevention. Accessed November 25, 2022. https://www.cdc.gov/museum/timeline/covid19.html.

de la Peña McCook, Kathleen. *Introduction to Public Librarianship*, 2nd ed. New York: Neal-Schuman, 2011.

Druin, Allison. "The Role of Children in the Design of New Technology," *Behaviour and Information Technology (BIT)* 27, no. 1 (2002): 1–25. https://doi.org/10.1080/01449290110108659.

Edmonds, M. Leslie. "From Superstition to Science: The Role of Research in Strengthening Public Library Service to Children," *Library Trends* 35, no. 3 (1987): 509–20. https://core.ac.uk/download/pdf/4816833.pdf.

Elizarova, Olga, and Kimberly Dowd. "Participatory Design in Practice." UX Magazine. October 14, 2017. https://uxmag.com/articles/participatory-design-in-practice.

Evans, Richard L. *Jean Piaget: The Man and His Ideas.* Translated by Eleanor Duckworth. New York: E. P. Dutton & Co., Inc., 1973.

Everyday Advocacy. "Identify Key Stakeholders." American Library Association, April 10, 2013. https://www.ala.org/everyday-advocacy/engage/identify-key-stakeholders.

Fenwick, Sara Innis. "Library Service to Children and Young People." *Library Trends* 25, no. 1, (1976): 329–60. http://hdl.handle.net/2142/6892.

Haas, Jessica C. "Blog: Event Planning Checklist." Programming Librarian, August 9, 2017. https://programminglibrarian.org/blog/event-planning-checklist.

Hill, Linda A., Greg Barbandeau, Emily Truelove, and Kent Lineback. *Collective Genius: The Art and Practice of Leading Innovation.* Boston, MA: Harvard Business Review Press, 2014. Kindle.

Historic Louisiana, Missouri. "Louisiana Public Library." Accessed March 7, 2023. https://historic-la-mo.com/historic-buildings/louisiana-public-library/.

IDEO. *Design Thinking for Libraries: A Toolkit for User-centered Design.* 2015. http://designthinkingforlibraries.com/toolkit.

Interactive Design Foundation. "What Is Design Thinking?" Accessed November 25, 2022. https://www.interaction-design.org/literature/topics/design-thinking#:~:text=Design%20thinking%20is%20an%20iterative%2C%20non%2Dlinear%20process%20which%20focuses,%2C%20Ideate%2C%20Prototype%20and%20Test.

International Federation of Library Associations and Institutions. "Our History." Accessed November 6, 2022. https://www.ifla.org/history/.

International Federation of Library Associations and Institutions. "Our Vision and Mission." Accessed November 6, 2022. https://www.ifla.org/vision-mission/.

Jbrary. "We Wave Our Scarves Together: Storytime Song." YouTube Video, 1:49. https://www.youtube.com/watch?v=HvnQP2z7Z9M.

Keats, Ezra Jack. *Peter's Chair.* New York: Picture Puffin Books, 1967.

Lambert, Megan Dowd. *Reading Picture Books with Children: How to Shake Up Storytime and Get Kids Talking About What They See.* Watertown, MA: Charlesbridge, 2015.

The Learning Groove. "Head, Shoulders, Knees and Toe." Accessed November 25, 2022. https://www.thelearninggroove.com/head-shoulders-knees--toes.

Lepper, Mark R., and David Greene. "Turning Play into Work: Effects of Adult Surveillance and Extrinsic Rewards on Children's Intrinsic Motivation." *Journal of Personality and Social Psychology* 31, no. 3 (1975): 479–86.

Meyers, Elaine, and Harriet Henderson. "Overview of Every Child Ready to Read @ Your Library, 1st edition." Accessed September 25, 2022. http://everychildreadytoread.org/overview-of-every-child-ready-to-read-your-library-1st-edition/.

Milto, Elissa, Meredith Portsmore, Jessica Watkins, Mary McCormick, and Morgan Hynes. *Novel Engineering, K–8: An Integrated Approach to Engineering and Literacy.* Arlington, VA: NSTA Press, 2020.

"Mister Rogers' Neighborhood," IMDb, accessed March 1, 2023, https://www.imdb.com/title/tt0062588/.

Montiel-Overall, Patricia. "Toward a Theory of Collaboration for Teachers and Librarians," *School Library Media Research* 8 (2005): 1–31. https://www.ala.org/aasl/sites/ala.org.aasl/files/content/aaslpubsandjournals/slr/vol8/SLMR_TheoryofCollaboration_V8.pdf.

Mooney, Carol. *Theories of Childhood.* St. Paul, MN: Redleaf Press, 2013. Hoopla.

Murray, Stuart A.P., The Library: An Illustrated History. New York: Skyhorse Publishing, 2009.

Museum of Play. "Educational Philosophy." Accessed November 25, 2022. https://www.museumofplay.org/educators/philosophy/.

National Impact of Library Public Programming Assessment. "About." Accessed November 25, 2022. https://nilppa.org/about/.

National Playing Fields. *Best Play: What Play Provisions Should Do for Children.* London: National Playing Fields Association, 2000. http://www.freeplaynetwork.org.uk/pubs/bestplay.pdf.

Nicholson, Simon. "How NOT to Cheat Children: The Theory of Loose Parts," *Landscape Architecture* (October 1971): 30–34.

Oakleaf, Megan. *Academic Library Value: The Impact Starter Kit.* Syracuse, NY: Dellas Graphics, 2012.

Pathways. "How Kids Learn to Play: 6 Stages of Play Development." Accessed November 25, 2022. https://pathways.org/kids-learn-play-6-stages-play-development/.

Play and Playground Encyclopedia. "Jean Piaget." Accessed September 25, 2022. https://www.pgpedia.com/p/jean-piaget.

Play and Playground Encyclopedia. "John Dewey." Accessed September 25, 2022. https://www.pgpedia.com/d/john-dewey.

Play and Playground Encyclopedia. "Lev Vygotsky." Accessed September 25, 2022. https://www.pgpedia.com/v/lev-vygotsky.

Rankin, Carolynn, ed. *IFLA Guidelines for Library Services to Children Ages 0–18*, 2nd ed. Netherlands: IFLA Library Services to Children and Young Adults Section, 2018.

Reynolds, Peter H. *The Dot.* Somerville, MA: Candlewick Books, 2003.

Riede, Felix, Niels N. Johannsen, Anders Högberg, April Nowell, and Marlize Lombard. "The Role of Play Objects and Object Play in Human Cognitive Evolution and Innovation." *Evolutionary Anthropology*, 27, no. 1 (2018): 46–59. https://doi.org/10.1002/evan.21555.

Rooted in Play. "Adventure Playground History." Accessed November 25, 2022. https://www.rootedinplay.org/adventureplaygrounds#.

Sayers, Frances Clarke. "The American Origins of Public Library Work with Children." Graduate School of Library and Information Science. University of Illinois at Urbana-Champaign, 1963. 6–13.

Search Institute. "The Developmental Assets Framework." Accessed November 2022. https://www.search-institute.org/our-research/development-assets/developmental-assets-framework/.

Sheppard, B., K. Flinner, R. J. Norlander, and M. D. Fournier. *National Impact of Library Public Programs Assessment: Phase 1, A White Paper on the Dimensions of Library Programs & the Skills and Training for Library Program Professionals.* NewKnowledge Publication #IML.074.207.07. Chicago: American Library Association & New Knowledge Organization Ltd., 2019. https://nilppa.org/wp-content/uploads/2019/06/NILPPA_Phase-1-white-paper.pdf.

Subramaniam, Mega, and Linda W. Braun. "Changing the Mindset of Pre-Service Librarians: Moving from Library Servants to Public Servants." IDEALS, ALISE 2021 Juried Papers. Published September 20, 2021. http://hdl.handle.net/2142/11093.

Subramaniam, Mega, Linda W. Braun, S. Nisa Asgarali-Hoffman, Keaunu Jordan-Stovall, and Christie Kodama. *Library Staff as Public Servants: A Field Guide for Preparing to Support Communities in Crisis.* College Park, MD: University of Maryland, Winter 2021. https://yxlab.ischool.umd.edu/projects/reimagining-youth-services-during-crises/.

Swann, Jr., William B., and Thane S. Pittman, "Initiating Play Activity of Children: The Moderating Influence of Verbal Cues on Intrinsic Motivation," *Child Development* 48, no. 3 (September 1977): 1128–32. https://doi.org/10.2307/1128374.

Taylor, Tim. *A Beginner's Guide to Mantle of the Expert: A Transformative Approach to Education.* Norwich, UK: Singular Publishing, 2016. Kindle.

Thomas, Fannette H. "The Genesis of Children's Library Services in the American Public Library, 1876–1906." Phd diss. University of Wisconsin–Madison, 1982. As quoted in Kathleen de la Peña McCook. *Introduction to Public Librarianship*, 2nd ed. New York: Neal Schuman, 2011.

Tullet, Hervé. *Press Here.* San Francisco, CA: Chronicle Books, 2011.

UNICEF. "Convention on the Rights of the Child." Accessed November 6, 2022, https://www.unicef.org/child-rights-convention/convention-text#.

University of Oregon. "Adventure Playground: Children Find Fun and Social Structure in World War 2 Bomb Site Rubble." YouTube Video, 13:52. https://www.youtube.com/watch?v=Uwj1wh5k5PY&t=2s.

YOUMedia Learning Labs Network. "What Is HOMAGO?" Accessed July 19, 2022. https://youmedia.org/about/homago/.

Index

adventure playgrounds, 74
ALSC; *See* Association of Library Services to Children
American Library Association (ALA), 2–3, 67, 74, 99
Association of Library Services to Children (ALSC), 3, 27, 74, 81

collaboration, models of, 62; collaboration, 66; cooperation, 63; coordination, 62; integrated instruction, 65–66
Connected Learning Alliance, 97
COVID-19 (pandemic), ix, xv, 33–34, 46, 68, 84

design thinking, x, 49–51, 54, 56, 58–59, 67, 82, 89, 92–93, 97; define, 49, 55; empathize, 49, 53, 70, 82, 97; ideate, 49; ideation, 49, 55–56; prototype, 49, 57–59, 92–94, 96; test, 49, 58–59, 89, 93, 96–98, 114
Dewey, John, 12

Erikson, Erik, 12, 14–16
Every Child Ready to Read (ECRR), 27–28

Ferguson, Missouri, xiii, xv, 24, 33, 36 81–82, 91–92, 112, 114, 117
Ferguson Municipal Library, 87
Ferguson Parks and Recreation, xiii, 59
Florissant, Missouri, xiii, 58, 91
Florissant Parks and Recreation, xiii, 59

Heathcote, Dorothy, 19
HOMAGO, 40

Institute of Museum and Library Services (IMLS), xiv, 42, 99
International Federation of Library Associations and Institutions (IFLA), 4–6

lap time (lap-sit), 13–15, 104
library program, definition of, 99
loose parts, 23–24
Louisiana, Missouri, x,xiii, 2, 51–53, 112, 129

Missouri State Library, xiv, 42
Montessori, Maria, 12, 16–17

National Institute of Library Public Programming Assessment (NILPPA), 99–100

National Playing Fields Association, 74
Novel Engineering, 28-29

open-ended play, definition, 23

Piaget, Jean, 12–18, 20
play, stages of, 85
playground, definition of, 73
playwork, 74–77
Public Library Association (PLA), 27

Rogers, Fred, xi, 18–19

school media specialist, 62–63, 65
SMART goals, 90–92
St. Louis County Library, x, xi, xiv, 24

story time, 6, 13, 15–16, 25–28, 41, 52–53, 58, 62, 65, 75, 84, 95, 101–104, 107–108
summer reading club, 43, 62–64, 66, 100
Syracuse University, xii, 129

Teen Advisory Group (TAG), 39, 93, 101, 106

United Nations Conventions on the Rights of the Child, 4

Vygotsky, Lev, 12, 17–18

Whole Book Approach, 27

Young Adult Library Services Association (YALSA), 3, 51

About the Author

Jennifer Ilardi was born and raised in the beautiful river town of Louisiana, Missouri, with her parents and three sisters. Growing up, she was involved with various community activities, including theater and school sports. She graduated from high school and went to Maryville University in St. Louis, Missouri, to study psychology. While there, she also became involved in the campus community through theater and residential life.

Jennifer has been able to work in a variety of environments from fast food and pizza places to interning at a movie studio in Manhattan, New York, and working as an assistant at a wildflower farm on Nantucket Island. Working at the public library as a youth services specialist was a unique way to blend customer service experience, theater, and an interest in helping young people. After working in the library for six years and attending as many professional development opportunities as she could get permission to attend, she decided to go to graduate school for library and information science at Syracuse University.

Graduate school gave Jennifer a broader perspective about the role of libraries and, more specifically, the librarians who operate the organization. Meeting and engaging with different graduate students from all over the country was insightful and enlightening. It was even more empowering when she enrolled in a post-graduate certificate program in Youth Experience at the University of Maryland. The education at these universities was challenging, but being among individuals who shared their passion about different aspects of the library helped her feel more comfortable in expressing her own passion for the power of libraries for communities and young people.

About the Author

When she isn't working to connect families and young people to information through her work as an instructor for homeschooling families or at Simple Positive Play, the organization she founded, she hangs out with her pet cat, daughter, and husband at home in Wentzville, Missouri.

www.ingramcontent.com/pod-product-compliance
Lightning Source LLC
Chambersburg PA
CBHW020748230426
43665CB00009B/534